AF570757

OTHER BOOKS BY CLAYTON ESHLEMAN

– Poetry –

Mexico & North (1962)
Indiana (1969)
Altars (1971)
Coils (1973)
The Gull Wall (1975)
What She Means (1978)
Nights We Put the Rock Together (1980)
Hades in Manganese (1981)
Fracture (1983)
The Name Encanyoned River: Selected Poems 1960–1985 (1986)
Hotel Cro-Magnon (1989)
Under World Arrest (1994)

– Prose –

Antiphonal Swing: Selected Prose 1960–1985 (1989)
Novices: A Study of Poetic Apprenticeship (1989)

–Translations –

Pablo Neruda, *Residence on Earth* (1962)
César Vallejo, *The Complete Posthumous Poetry*
(with José Rubia Barcia, 1978)
Aimé Césaire, *The Collected Poetry* (with Annette Smith, 1983)
Michel Deguy, *Given Giving* (1984)
Bernard Bador, *Sea Urchin Harakiri* (1986)
Conductors of the Pit (1988)
Aimé Césaire, *Lyric & Narrative Poetry 1946–1982*
(with Annette Smith, 1990)
César Vallejo, *Trilce* (1992)
Antonin Artaud, *Watchfiends and Rack Screams*
(with Bernard Bador, 1995)

– Editor –

Folio (Bloomington, Indiana, 3 issues, 1959–1960)
Quena (Lima, Peru, 1 issue, published and suppressed by
the North American Peruvian Cultural Institute, 1966)
Caterpillar (NYC–Los Angeles, 20 issues, 1967–1973)
A Caterpillar Anthology (material from issues #1–12,
Doubleday, NYC, 1971)
Sulfur (Pasadena–Los Angeles–Ypsilanti, 42 issues, 1981–1998)

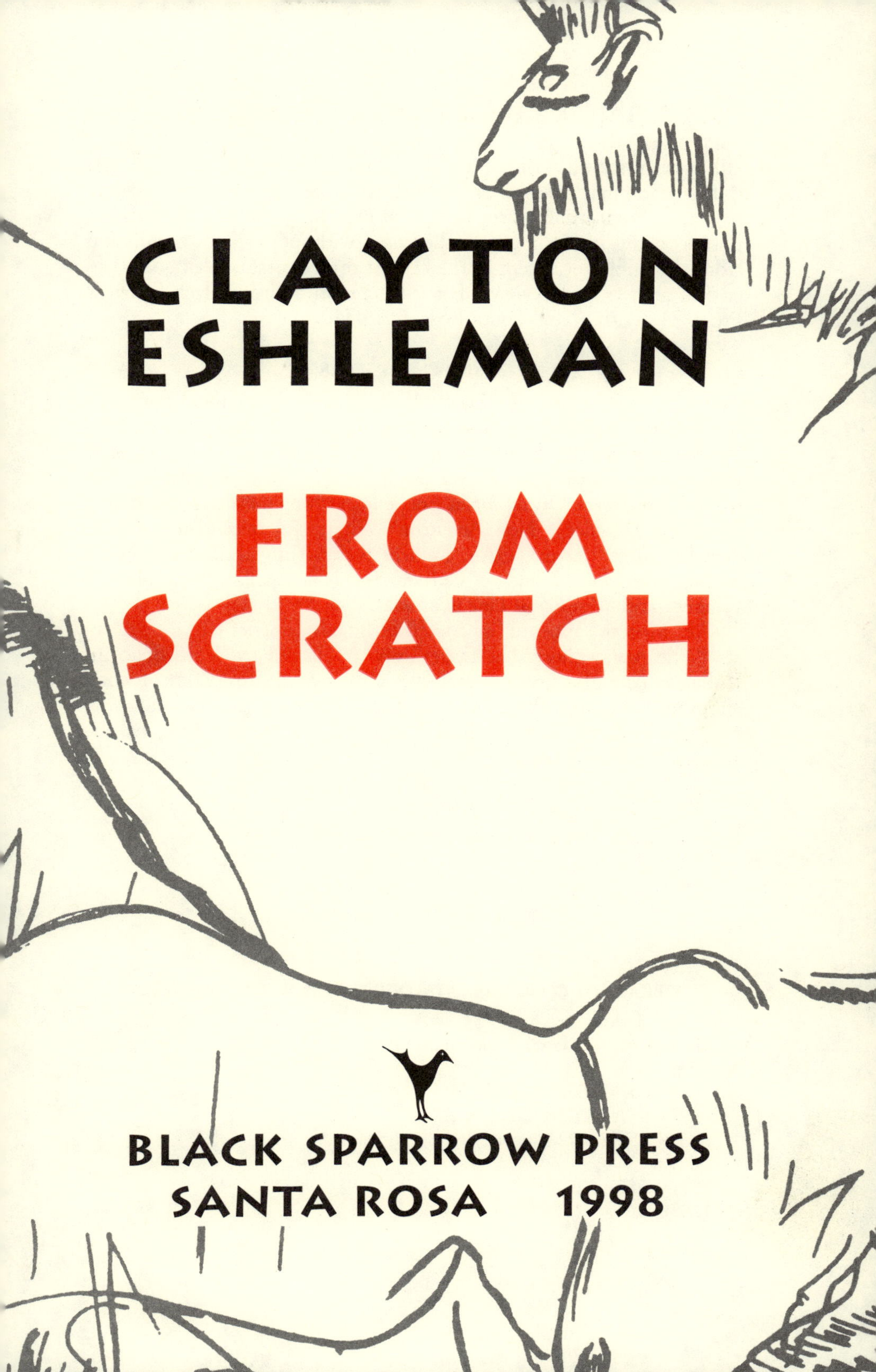

CLAYTON ESHLEMAN

FROM SCRATCH

BLACK SPARROW PRESS
SANTA ROSA 1998

FROM SCRATCH. Copyright © 1998 by Clayton Eshleman.

All rights reserved. Printed in the United States of America. No part of this book may be used or reproduced, stored in a retrieval system, or transmitted, in any form or by any means, electronic, mechanical, photocopying, recording or otherwise, without written permission from the publisher except in the case of brief quotations embodied in critical articles and reviews. For information address Black Sparrow Press, 24 Tenth Street, Santa Rosa, CA 95401.

ACKNOWLEDGMENTS

Many of these poems (occasionally in different versions) appeared in the following magazines: *American Letters & Commentary, Apex of the M, The Baffler, Bombay Gin, Boxkite* (Australia), *BullHead, The Cafe Review, FlashPoint, Grand Street, Graffiti Rag, Hambone, Heat* (Australia), *House Organ, Japan Environment Monitor, Letter, Lusitania, Mandorla* (Mexico), *New American Writing, no roses, Paris Review, Printed Matter* (Japan), *QAE, Radical Poetics* (England), *Sugar Mule, Sulfur, Terra Nova: Nature & Culture, Trembling Ladders* (Australia), *X Connect*, and *West Coast Line* (Canada).

"El Mozote" appeared as *BullHead Broadside Series #1.*

"The Atmosphere, Les Eyzies" was published by Word Space in Dallas as part of a promotional flyer for a two-day residency of workshops and readings: *Poetic Descents: Excursions with Clayton Eshleman.*

"Nora's Roar" was published as the book, *Nora's Roar,* by the Rodent Press in Boulder, 1996.

Black Sparrow Press books are printed on acid-free paper.

LIBRARY OF CONGRESS CATALOGING-IN-PUBLICATION DATA

Eshleman, Clayton.
From scratch / Clayton Eshleman.
p. cm.
ISBN 1-57423-070-0 (paperback)
ISBN 1-57423-071-9 (cloth trade)
ISBN 1-57423-072-7 (signed cloth)
I. Title.
PS3555.S5F75 1998
811'.54—dc21

98-24441
CIP

for Caryl

this juniper fuse

TABLE OF CONTENTS

from Scratch

PROLEGOMENA

Golgonooza, William Blake's City of Art, contained "all that has existed in the space of six thousand years"—Blake's back wall was Druidic-Neolithic. With the 20th century discovery of Upper Paleolithic imagination, specifically with the discovery of the Mousterian cupules at La Ferrassie, we must backdate Blake's "six thousand years" to "fifty thousand years"

•

With toe in mouth,
with serpent-encircled web

Who rests within,
circling within

Who slays weds fecundates

The desire to become conscious

    A point
wants to continue, can't
continues, pointilating about,
indenting

Grinding in, as if to make fire

A point expanding, a point blank
dent
appointing

Grinding out a cup shape in stone.

                As if turning over a log

and discovering the mucus-side of Eden,
Denis Peyrony "lifted it and turned it over. On the lower
face, in an angle of the smoothed surface, we noticed a
small cupule associated with a series of other cupules"
(he is at La Ferrassie in 1909,
excavating a Mousterian level, and has just turned over
a one meter triangular limestone slab
covering an egg-shaped grave pit
containing the remains of a child)

Over the Neandertal child's cranium I see the cupule
    become a dome,
the cathedral-to-be as the cave pulled upward inside-out
—the burial vault in the base of a pyramid
is the terminal form of the cave,
the space in which immortality is contested

Cupuled slab and egg-shaped pit
an alchemical vessel
containing the stuff of resurrection?

Depressed is raised, what is above is below

"I now am what I am: a horror and an astonishment"

I got hot and became pregnant,
I could feel the sun rising through my diaphragm

With the tongs of my tongue
I tore at my thought-heart

I ground rock out of rock,
this waste was my food

"And they builded Golgonooza: terrible eternal labour!"

I

REVERBERATIONS

Our journey had ceased to advance.
At that odd fork
we sensed the eternity we had spurned.
Being now led
everywhere, nowhere. Our journey into the fork
was molecular—a gate in every god
led only into cities of the dying,
to no cities of the dead.
Retreat seemed the only hope,
yet behind was ice,
the sphincter of a mastodon
a ragged halo in the fogged and snarling air.
Thus did we dig in here
as if below held a larger here
uncleaved by journey's division
inherent in every route.

•

There is a portion of the night
unlike port or storm, a gash
ribbed red, as if lit
with under fire, in which I am known
all around, seen through
as if with crossing spots.
Each organ has a faceless nave
leading to an altar absence
through which the world is rolling.
Being, weighed, is superstructure.
And "not"? Rim of the almost
tender night's containment.

•

Caught red-handed with the dawn,
I strained to see my catcher
masked, who thus received me
as sunlight re-sieves the lawn

Deknowing had begun. The space between
predator and prey, I, Protean,
vanished as the curve sunk home:
pitcher balling spills of pitchers spilling fills.

•

Were one woman to tell the truth about her life,
Muriel Rukeyser wrote, the world would split open.
Rigoberta Menchu—did you lie?

Or does the world split instantly
while men retie and splice?

•

The snow as a sorcery
of air, to bevel and conceal
what we know of here:
that it is blank
at summer core,
without possessive,
a "t" away from there.
As if the dark
intensified were white,
and whiteness fully brought to light
the matrix springs of night.

AFTER READING ACKROYD'S *BLAKE*

There is no place in which imagination
can rest: take my father—
still do I see him in Nazi armband raking leaves,
I watch him now from the Rimbaud porthole,
he's an oily swirl of autumnal colors
clawing at the flesh of the earth.
In the back of his head a beacon pours yellow light
through the rooms of 4705. I see the egg clusters on the walls,
the hives and bubbling sacs,   organic 4705
less a dwelling than a structure—
my mother slowly flaps through, a weeping manta ray
in an underworld of Biblical directives.
My father has just harvested several Negro children
who tried to pick up his precious fallen buckeyes.
He bound and gagged them, kept them in jars for months.
Sparky has been thrashed. I've been whipped.
How move into a statement on the nature of God?
I hold a globe of father-semen in my palm,
mold it into a grigri, then send it spinning into
the buckeye's crown. All perils have direct access to
the basement of man, where the chains and harrows
turn, and the Giant Forms one's parents are
move like the heads of mastodons through bottomless
vales of mist. The tusk face of my mother
now opens too, I see her Pandoric dilemma,
her terrible lack of confidence, doubt
like anatomical rift. I see my father
try to befriend me without knowing how.
He walks strapped to the frame of his father's vise.
Ancestral bellows pumped through him may end here.

DE KOONING'S *WOMAN I*

is the first in a series, probably not
in de Kooning's sense of it primal woman or
first—earliest—woman, but these facets may have been
on his mind, for we have here a series of "ones,"
a sacrificed and dismembered "goddess,"
a kind of North American Coyolxauhqui
whose circular Stone was discovered at the foot of the Great
   Temple stairway,
as well as Madonna and Child,
the Child at once just born and maybe four,
he is bald and white, is the Madonna's left shoulder and arm,
staring at Her, perched on what appears to be
Her ruddy left thigh, which
on closer inspection might also be
the rump of a flat-snouted or headless animal
lunging to the right, whose back and legs are Her lap and legs,
lunging into the shredding legs of the figure who uses
the Madonna's right shoulder and arm as his breast and stomach
(which is also a red-gartered, chubby, severed thigh)—
he has long, loosely-tied hair, or is "he" a midwife
with face hair—a pirate? sniffing
or whispering to the Madonna's right temple?
His breast-stomach is also his right arm
swinging under the Madonna's haltered and huge right breast,
and out of his splitting hand
another hand emerges from which
shears protrude cutting the Child's umbilicus?
Or is a castration under way?

All this action is simultaneously
splintered and frozen,
once we see the Child, the animal, and pirate-midwife,
there's not much left of *Woman I,* or

let's say she's in sacrificial drag,
all but her head and breasts are others
masquerading as her body parts,
she is a crowned tripod of wedge-head and dome-shielded breasts,
dismembered *and* whole? or have her body parts been stuffed into
new roles?
Over-sized Mesopotamian eyes, hypnotic,
teeth like a portcullis   beaver-set into her face,
the gaze of one who has been blasted,
the left eye straight ahead,
as wide open animal jaws howl at her earless head,
the right eye more inward, averted,
reflecting on what pirate-midwife is hissing—

to her left, beyond the Child,
a sketchy, wraith-like creature, at attention,
facing her, seems to be tooting or snout-firing into her face,
or is he vying for her attention with pirate-midwife?
She whose body is her retinue,
She who is slaughtered
at the beginning of time, sets time in motion,
whose crate-shaped upper body
contains, like huge pods, food for those
putting on her body,
it is hideous,
and magnificent,
"Huitzilopochtli
cut off her head,
which was left abandoned
on the slopes of Coatepetl.
The body of Coyolxauhqui
went rolling down
as it fell, dismembered,
in different places fell her hands,
her legs, her body..."

“Like a black hole in space,
which destroys all light around it
but somehow gives rise to galaxies,
sacrifice is a vacuum at the center of culture
which somehow spins the web of life.”

THIS DICTIONARY IS MY FATHER'S BOOK.
I crocodiled it from him.
My baby bottom flashed
the horror of the moon

These words are my father's lords.
I enspeculated them from him.
My puberty flexed
as his whip raved wild

These words are my father's gnomes.
I listened to my dog's death.
Sparky's maggots formed
the ordered chaos of my lines

These words are my father's failure
to rule. These words are my mother lore,
this is the blitz of my father,
I am steeped in his unspeakable hell.

THE THING IS, TO REMAIN IN NIGREDO

all   stages active, at once,
progression, but only that which comes
   with experience of the art,
            in the art—in the aft
                  of the art,
its stern sail,   it is in the behind of ourselves
         where we learn,
and if you do not learn—
   but here I am, in absolute, again.
One must learn,
but learning, like experience, is not a progression,
the earliest rudiments, and the keenest solutions,
   intermingle

         one steps out into the spring
         night air,   toxic with wailing sirens,
                        confused buds—
the toxin is me,   one must say,
I am responsible for this minute of mine on the planet.
   —which is not true,
but so true
      one's flesh falls away.

SELF-PORTRAIT BY A CAMEROON MASK

crowned with octopi?
—a bowl-like rack of lizards,
synchronized to unsocket god power,
mask crawling with masks,
whose forehead is a pregnant belly,
nose   a penis with almond eye testicles,
cheeks   taut breasts—

it is time to become a squid-jawed ant!
to smoke my oldest umbilicus,
inhaling the sunrise archaics
packed in midnight's ebony

I've always looked to myself
too much like I look,
intentional, calm, forced about the edges,
comic in fracture, loving,
judgmental, pissed under my eyes,
concerned, too cautious...

[Musée National des Arts
d'Afrique et d'Océanie, Paris]

MUDRA

I have taken off the Vallejo ring,
have stripped myself of predecessor,
held
up to the light this circle of doubt,
letting my 4th finger recall solely
the distant thumb,
prehistoric
inspring of paw and maw.

•

To inter the predecessor in a word.

•

I have taken off the spider ring,
have set
aside my turquoise, my leggy silver—
last piece of armor, last
breloque.
The witherlines streaking through my hand
leap the ring loss.

INTENTION

To write
as a sculptor carves, cutting a way to the unknown,
contextualizing the locust raid of the subconscious,
to form caves within the line,
alcoves within sentences, to inhabit the line
a string of nomadic campfires
stretching through the karst,

a braiding,
something I admire in Celan, in Bracho,
a motive roaming, redolent with, adding
to, the matrix linking

Dream of sleigh-bells attached to Death's roller-coaster spine

Who knows why autumn cracks
and corrects our core? The gold is already
rafting in each leaf Medusa
flowers.

UNLEAVING

I threw myself on the leaf-strewn ground,
under the red maple I've watched grow 10 years
I wished the earth would take off,
a roving mastodon, with me clutched–
instead, I fisted leaves and rolled
up to the trunk, a newborn pup
up to a teat, I put a star in my mouth
counted its milky rays
then slid down the nightside of Eden
into the tunnels that gap the underworld ...

Who will read the fallen leaves?   not in tea
but in drift,   who will read
the urn of death? I see patches of its sides

coiling shreds the raising wind spits ...

A dress of leaves for one who is ashes ...

Each leaf a tiny tree of vascular bundles,
litterings that lift
the unappeasable need for inspiration,
for nothing's abstract concreteness,
the end of the world telescoped into the now
inconceivable beginning,
millennial patience casting anchor as it crests

Imagine this wet scat,
the "wanwood leafmeal" of these photosynthetic factories: "under the influence of light, six molecules of carbon dioxide combine with six of water to produce one molecule of sugar and six of oxygen. This single molecule of sugar ... is the basis of life."
                                        Say that the maple

produces leaves to feed itself, that they know
to unleave when no longer needed.
I am creating something to feed me:
serene blue-bellied hornets
drag their rickshaws out of repressed sheds
to the shores of Lake Gargoylalia,
they hover, waiting for the mutilated to be coughed up,
the lake belches, and like swans
robed in oily mist the bodies toss,
a few are speared and rickshaw deposited,
and now ticks and cockchafers get in line,
and thoughtchafers, a caterpillar confetti,
the vertebral thunder of a nest of dead leaves,
the abyss encapsulated in the Western God
whose African children are worm bores,
bags of glassy sore flows,
monstrous blending of all images
as I shuffle through these newsreels—
carotenoid thrust of Kali
shutting down chlorophyll,
and is not Shiva the purplescent meaty luster
in the still scarlet and violet oak?
There is a moment in every autumn
when angel is unzipped from watchfiend,
an unleaving,   when remaining is letting go.
Persephone takes the erect invisible into her throat,
the icy but still igneous breeze
is the onset of Hades' ejaculation,
the snow to come, its lees.

II

Nora's Roar

In Memory of Nora Jaffe
(1928–1994)

❐

As she recedes, living still,
first lung, now liver,
I am turning to
"The everlasting eyes of Pierrot
And, of Gargantua, the laughter"
                her laugh
Ohio Gothic, bass
swoons, a booming of merriment,
   we lay in the dawn road pickled
while others dropped salt into our mouth

To wake and to think only of the wine to come,
the wine of the work of drawing,
to need only this wine, to live
in near obscurity, happy
within the frame of imagination, this word
we mob,

it is our only refuge.

[7 October, 1994]

❐

the wake an elegy stirs ... something to be listened to.
I find you everywhere, mainly as voice echo,
I think of you, then hear you before I see
entoptically a blur of your face ...

the unheard voice then resilences. The silence
opens out, chimes of *Habilis, Erectus* ...
  the wake of elegy, dirty churn of what
            the voyage rejected,
standing at the stern of what life might be,
it keeps you pinned in me, as I pine,
semi-conscious unplugging of a bathtub
in which the water used doesn't want to leave ...

❐

Most just, I guess, to find you
in the flux of realization and grief.
As ash, you are a complete whatever,
and it is hard to comprehend that anti-force.
I string it on my feeling for you

to go overboard with you,
to honor your rich void.
I am gaining this word by word,
for the loss is at odds
with something curdled in praise.
The grand "So What" flicks by,
at Miles Davis with my need to bulge
absence/presence

"Sadness" once meant "solidity,"
"steadfastness in faith,"
but nothing will support my sadness this week,
          a wandering distraction, as if
Nora's death were a jellyfish box
   adrift in my atmosphere.
Death has four sets of eyes, no brain,
one set for each side of what we call direction.
Death's mouth is over its eyes...

my sadness is layered, pillow-like, or tarps
   with pillows pressed between,
moistened but not drenched, stranded
      adrift... as all senses of her
cancel, recompose,
        "Procession of the Quick"

The upward piling impulse of eternity. Cloud-like, rock-like, forms, jostling against—here it comes again—absolute absence

A leg, thigh and calf, bent, lower left hand corner, gets me interested in the physicality, the eros? of the painting, now I spot a male back lunging upward, whose head disappears in a kind of window of winter trees. His right arm droops, leading me to a woman—it's Nora herself!—eyeballs rolled up, hair stark black and funnel-like swooping into the upper right corner

The work now looks draped, an upward piling, weighted, with loose, body-like forms, detonated below, into floating, bumping, somewhat phallic blocks—on which the rest of the painting "stands" —it doesn't really stand, it wobbles, tectonic, as if on plates? (suddenly the buttocks of the upward lunging male look like an amazed lion!)

The form argues, wrestles with, the punctilio of human desire salted, as ground, for a realization of the form to *grind against.* Nora Jaffe depicts herself under a roving blank cloak of men, as they surge around, across, and over her. The procession of the quick, *being* overwhelmed, as the quick (and the dead?) pile into paradise, over the body of the painter—

Cocks abound, but as often in Jaffe they are syntactical eels, the patriarchal thrashing in the net of an imagination that instead of practicing political correctness prefers, demands, the re-leasing of the obsession. Coils of rape are here bounded but not dismissed—

the out-of-in-balance of the painting amazes me. I'm stuck
with the use of the female (Nora) body overlayed by blankets
(lacunae) of quasi-phallics. Now I lay me down to sleep.
The garment of the world: stitched penises. O
mother: where? As the garment out of which the cocks are stitched.
O father: why? Isn't it wonderful how semi-abstract,
charged and essentially formal works dump our psyche
upward? My father made me a blanket out of my mother, ay!

then withdrew it, leaving me with my first tooth!
oh! and it is around this tooth that I have woven my poems,
weave, woven, sploven ... the spindle bursts,
yet a King now appears at the crest of "Procession of the Quick"
—the winter landscape is his crown,
his body that of the lunging man,
willynilly covering the now double female body
(two heads, Nora's and what I took to be another man's)
and he is kind of dancing, as he fucks,
lifting a Subcommandante Marcos leg, as an insult to
all fashion, as a shark form noses in ...

But why two women? Why both at once?

We are in orgy at every moment (too many unused parts)

❒

This sadness is without edge
or forceps, it is weighted with total absence,
which is the difference
between Nora's ashes, and Nora,   it can be
weighed in mind, it is fractal
and thus not without contour,
it is the toothed heart of a black hole,
what the star feels in its inexhaustible extinction ...

Sadness, then, is a protection,
a kind of Covering Harem,
it is sweet, as "The Wild Rose" in Budapest was sweet,
nostalgia mired in cool fat, a piano player
whose elderly foetal head, with stuff oozing onto the keyboard,
smiled at us, the eaters,
jellyfish box abob ...

Our friendship was blessed with an erotic lining.
My eyes turned off before Nora's art
and something else turned on—
a glade would appear, compact male flesh
reorganized, penis shifted to armpit,
thigh used three ways, as stalagmite, Long Island, floe,
libido frozen, on the trail of her hand
finding its way through a coral forest of congealed
male fragmentation

Seeing the extent to which
she had imagined her masculine-fraught destiny,
I knew male force was grasped, and that she was free
—for a moment. We can deal with nearly anything
—for a moment. In minuscule time,
a stroke, or an image, is paradise,

darkness a chrysalis of unharvested stars

She had reorganized the male tentacles
and glimpsed what Bosch envisioned
—while she smoked.
In her breath, steel doors began to rot.
She hurt herself
as who does not who has glimpsed the other as
"Dear Fellow Particle"?

It is very transpersonal, never private,
how the pylon figures of our lives
rub open scars and palpitate the antique
  feeling under,
another flesh, which the pylon detects

Nora is Egyptian,
a gorgeous baboon
in whose slender figure my language
is hived.

❐

To learn to love your death.
Is this not the requirement? not to love death,
but to love you in death,
to learn nourishment from your absence

Dear now ancestral spirit, you feed me
as do the spirits of poets dead but for the page,
or frame, of chaos, white
for these ant legions

Are not the chosen dead blowing
energy into these lines? Yes, I have good energy,
but it is nothing compared to
Nora as ash, the microscopic gale
    in the thought of her,

billowing, these dead who make life-in-image possible,
we all work at a single world poem,
    a hybrid exchange,
I become pregnant with Nora's soul,
I swell at night, cannot rest, I sleep
      but do not rest...

how beautifully herbs break in, fumes and
filterings, by which her presence is
swarming, micron by micron, with the jest of absence,
        like tiny wine flies...

Nora's spell,   terrible to be a speck in this exchange.

❐

As she rises, or seems to hold,
while rising, the anaconda
tree trunk, *writhe,*
rise, it is the sound of whiteness,
as she pulleys up, her right
hand spider-walks the trunk,
making a lingam: combined
arm hand trunk,
                                        as she rises
in place, out of the fern
white, her rising is
white infested,
                                      mascara
no pupils
(work this also in:
work her hood in, her head
held to the tree, to
anaconda white
speckled
bark,
        the phallus was
what she could put inside her of
the tree, up inside her
the bandaged
anaconda, I under-
stand now,
                    it was the trunk
she loved, the sap
in its bark helmet, the serpentine.

❒

A hardon, severed,
enwombed, the umbilical-
knotted
goad

Nut
descends, arms
alongside,
she kisses its cleft, tongues

the semen-charged

mummification,

the hydra-hydrant
gong.

❐

One senses in her art a luxuriant ambivalence
toward masculinity,
"Merman" manticore pushing into female
plush, the tobacco
in the cigarette, dildo
as driving void,   a sort of infant

misericordia, this 9 inch nail
rubbery as old celery
has been given refuge,

battered Manhattan, bandaged, as a lingam,
with potato-eyes, ending in a hoof,

"Our Strips of Stuff"
lingam bound to stretcher poles,
bags of blood, bound in with coal and stones,

whose yoni is a nurse
whose ward (whose nave)
strains with mayhem chained,

gorgeous energy, this
crest of a house ridge phallic helmet line
whose attic is timbered meat.

❐

The dirtiness of death,
        her head a chopped meadow,
chemo-crewcut grey and stubby,
steroid swollen face. I did not recognize Nora,
blundered into the next death section
        CLAYTON   I heard my voice
This man in her bed—then knew he was Nora,
who asked me to bring her a box of Malomars.
Because of the steroids, she said, she would wake at 4 AM
   ravenous   (perhaps also to see me
                    one last time...

I cannot say what was in the bedpan,
I would like to,   to keep my poetry
sensitive to what we suffer,
or what was in the casket
no casket,   ash,   her goings,
the butchered countenance and what must be
   wrapped, discarded,
            O I am thinking, Charles
Baudelaire, into the fluttery life of your old ones,
as they snapped like wasps against the rue corner,
is this an indulgence
   or is it touched with cancer?

Must poetry become infected to truly live?

❐

October 30, 1994
Día de los muertos

Is it possible there are better days in Bardo
than others? Days of less weighing, days of more
rending? Nora on one scalepan ash,
on the other, a speculum mirroring the heart.

Could I recognize you in Bardo,
I would have to love your shredded tentacles,
your eyes I once knew as piercing
now dead wash across some scene of disarticulation,
the paintings taken back into the experiences
out of which they came, so that Joe's face now
floods the periscope eyepiece

Forty days, is Bardo, is she being dressed?
Is she a trussed goat? Dressed for the pyramid?
Force-fed for sacrifice? What happens in these forty nights?
And then I saw them slam you down again
and take you apart

And then I saw them slam you down again
and take you apart

Forty days, is Bardo, is she being flayed?
Can they get her heart on the scales?
We project jealousy on even the caterpillar.
Rood into the sky of prehistory.
Subjectile man: we magnetize *and* we project

This is her day twenty-two.
For what does she battle in Bardo?

Release? She is released. To not come back?
She's back for a pause, lodged in my kale,
in the very nurture of my breathing

Drafting her battle, like I once drew her bath.

❐

The back of my head is hollow

it is filled with Nora's ash

                Nora ash
the possessive disappears.

❐

Nora's roar:

you're inside my body now
and while it may look like ash from without,
inside, in this drawing, this apart-ment,
these interlocking fuses, these cunei or cunt forms,
these uncials, my face is forever present,
forever as long as seen, perceived as my allegiance to Aphrodite,
the line, the point of the line on the long and generous leash of
body as the enduring reality.
There is no significant form without body's roar,
the long and terrible adventure of two bodies,
three, four, woman in mother in man in father, two-by-fours,
unlock the cross and let its ties swarm—
you will not escape my body for I will not conform, be
formula, be line without body's presence.
And so, though I love a line more than line can aura,
for my love to be good it must scintillate with origin,
member, cavern of pools and dentata.
In this ever nearness to body is my joy—
body the unfolding interlock of generative stillness,
defused as the line, tender earthworm,
heads off into the loam of blankness again and in her curling,
in her feints, gasps, spurts, crests my love,
roars my forehead into galley, rowing, stroking deep,
tasting the lover as line tongue delirium into sense and
registers home.

❐

A jaguar of bubbles in the toilet bowl
tells me your Bardo
                                Flushed

and then an airplane,   as if company,
    hums against my lungs.

❐

"Beyond Repair," she said,
I want to paint a painting I could call
"Beyond Repair"

my mind honed on Indiana heard a wreck.
I fidgeted toward her meaning: a painting
that was *beyond* repair (hear: compare)–
    a painting no one could monkey with,
a painting that was beyond
      repair,

thus perfect, with no break-downable parts,
a painting no one
                                        could do better.
a flame beyond breath. no one can blow out.
smokeless. of air. liquid. a painting that would prove
    she is so here
no one could de Kooning her standing.
why not? she wants a painting that will last forever.
that no one will fuck with.
a painting that will blaze with her being.
that you can enter. in which you can be.
yes. blues for Nora.
she wants her essence to be attended.
she wants the pelvis to be. the pelvis fossil.
she wants man as *Homo* in, as *Erectus.*
she wants erect man to scream inside
      the downy glade pro-
nounced woman. she wants woman like a wagon train
to encircle innocence (Does she know
no one is innocent? Of course. she knows and
    does not know.
like us, the living who know less than she.

like the alive man who thinks he is alive.
and the poor dead woman who might think
 she is totally dead
TOTAL is the name of the station I took gas from tonight.
TOTAL is the 7 oil multinational sisters.
TOTAL the impact of capitalism on indigenous person.
 As blacks and whites swarm into the blues.
as the blue sky and blues and bruise fuse
a brilliant dim carpet on which Prufrock would never
 dare to recline—
against the total. of the total. yes. totaled one.

she wants all life to reign. pile. and scour.

III

NIGHTCRAWLERS

Last night it was not Ophelia but Nora Jaffe crawling the Milky Way, her cloud body shredding like Nancy Spero's image of a mutilated Salvadoran woman crawling the dirt on which she had been assaulted—and I thought of Rigoberta Menchu's mother crawling tethered to a tree, of Charles Olson describing himself as a "tireless Intichiuma eater & crawler of my own ground," of Gary Snyder off the trail crawling "on the crunchy manzanita leaf clover ... around between the trunks"—

as I continued to dream and reflect, I saw all these crawlers, one below the other, moving in parallel rhythm, some agonized, some studiously inspecting—all seemed to be returning to their totem, their *ototama* or *ototeman*, to their animal brothers or sisters, this nearly-destroyed blood-covenant between the human and the animal—

our night crawl through Le Tuc d'Audoubert, past bear skulls and viper skeletons, to the sculpted bison 700 meters inside the cave, made a vulva-like loop, a coming turning going, with the mating animals as the center—

and then there is the story my Indian friend in Bloomington told me in 1960: how on his first night there, having come directly to Indiana from India, he walked past a house on which there was a sign: *Nightcrawlers*. He was touched by what he thought was the kindness of Americans: hotels for drunks that stayed open all night long—

there are now other kinds of nightcrawlers, big tough ones moving across darkened Michigan firing-ranges, toward targets of silhouette men, the heart areas blown out. Upright around their smoking barbecues, my fellow Americans are singing: "Drop kick me, Jesus, through the goal posts of life!"

SHMATTE VARIATIONS

[based on the dolls
of Michel Nedjar]

Dolls as witnesses,
at a toll gate
through which nothing passes

or at the nothing toll
where something is always refused

•

Shmattess Annie,
"raggedy"
Indianapolis, 1941 (where I found my dolls
under the Christmas tree,
propped there in candy-striped
"poor children clothing")

•

"Beginners in the world, as we were, we could not feel superior to any thing except, at most, to such a half-object as this, given to us the way some broken fragment is given to creatures in aquariums, so that it may serve them as a measure and landmark in the world around them"

•

Nedjar, born in 1947, over
a deeply-embedded stinger,
a deportation burial, the root
disappearance of a daikon

whitened body,   shadow of family
    tailor floor cuttings
folded about a twig,   a first doll,
a variation on primal
        enwrapping

•

Of what does the spider dream?
A fanged vulva swirling with legs

Of what does the foetus dream?
A flounder is swimming within me

•

Through the Hiroshima horror, a Butoh mask.
Flea-market stage. Black bundles stuck to bridges.
A naked Japanese man, standing
in the rain, holding out his eyeball

Abyss as an *active* ingredient
in the "sweet
ginger and dynamite" of the mind

•

Heads packed in heads, insect-
perforated fabric. The head as nest,
a runny nest, as if in the twill
a human soul was pushing,
trapped,
                "blackened Athena"
the bubbly stitchwork grins

•

Of what does the spider dream?
Of little Miss Muffet
Of Muffet as curd
Of pupa dolls, of mummy pots
Of Last Suppers taking yugas to complete
Of the Crucified's stomach honey
Of eating as copulation, copulation as eating
Of orifices bowling through their bowels

•

Nedjar's dolls as wind scorpions:

"Courtship has seldom been witnessed. A female doll becomes cataleptic in response to stroking and tapping by the male who then opens the female genital orifice with his chelicerae. Having emitted a spectral globule of semen, he picks it up in his chelicerae and inserts it into the female. The female doll lays her eggs in a deep burrow in which she continues to live. The doll eggs hatch into six-legged larvae which eventually moult, acquiring a fourth pair of legs."

Or as sea spiders:

"The extreme reduction of the trunk and abdomen has resulted in organs such as the gut diverticula and ovaries being forced out into the legs."

REGISTER'S BEYOND
is a waiting room emptied of
the goitered masses. Even the aluminum has been
frisked. A water's edge,
peach rose silver blue,
pervades the earth and sky impasto

        Ruth Martin creeps past
on her walker. Soft hall rug.
Old bare feet, as if through Register's
beyond, before a milk turquoise
lake arrest, where
branchless smoke thins to trees.

•

All living
room is, in a way, a waiting
room for the beyond. In Register,
light is a chorus of rectangles,
squarings, frail, violet diagonals,
sometimes intersected by a chair actor

I write for the chairs, Jim Hillman remarked.
He had in mind the great dead
who he believed were present at yearly
Eranos Lectures, so that when he delivered
"The Thought of the Heart"
he addressed the presence of Jung, say,
or Freud, not those presently on the chairs

Register's chairs are unoccupied.
No one's in the waiting room.

We're all in the beyond?

A tenuous vinyl bucket "yes."
"You've gone on and left
as you are sitting here. No matter
how fast you zoom away from the Cadillac Hotel
you'll never overtake this leaving."

•

Insectile, shadow-feelered chairs.
Empty sandwich shop, panty pastel pink light.
Shiny blood red banquettes,
as if paused in chess, facing
a gameless formica tabletop.
Armless distortions of our mothers' arms,
as if beds had thrown off their mattresses
and, contracting, flexed–
receptacles for haunches.
Man sitting, half a swastika

Chair.
Cathedral.

•

Or are we yet to come?
Is Register's beyond the next second
we'd like to fill with expanded spirit?
My patience goes crazy before these lime
fast food plastic chairs,
heaping serpents on them
or slamming them through windows.

•

In the waiting room for the beyond
there are no rugs, no pictures.
In the airport plate-glass:
lavender-pale clouds like breakers.
A boundless anti-self,
absence as basis

The centered, vacant
chair issues two intersecting shadows:
it is wombed in tombal fortitude,
expanded in curtailment.

GIVERNY

Nasturtium surplus.
      Water curls and lilies,
lily water.   Vermilion and orange
flower flow, nearly stemming
          Monet's path,
the great division between
painting things and painting sensation.
If Yeats awakes one day,
this will all be virtual.   Tender
      green salad of the earth.
   Water curls and willows,
     a maggot belches

below the tourists' feet

No noun used to be safe here

A few roses trellis overhead

Mucilaginous quince.

DE KOONING'S *FEBRUARY*

The observational,
vanished, figures emerge,
as if by chance, through
a meeting of my projections and stroke
con*figur*ations. A Luba jaw
curve juts stops spurts up as if along a crossed-out
upper face. Khakis, sages,
swank with white. Flotsam from Soutine's Céret
assembled on a beach.
Only some "rope" and "ain't" are left from
European Painting. Raw paint, as if
we were in Mas d'Azil facing
rampant "macaroni," a penis, animal parts. Not
quite. Under de Kooning is a done-to-death tradition.
Under the Upper Paleolithic is no image.
The Aurignacians still have the floor.

A bronze erection on stilts
emerges from a rock shelter
whose space ejaculates light.
Waves evoked, taken away. Turner sea light,
Matta cosmogonic hints. Taken away.

The Luba jaw is also the front half of a grand piano,
the rear half of a peacock-blue bison.
This jaw-keyboard-rump is being played or
buggered by a sketchy ape with a feline face.
How curb a dog that's slowly exploding?
Spurting up jaw standing swab
tattered cloak swipe of grey-green mist
topped by white helmet-shaped woman's hair.
Is "she" holding out a mangled gold foetus?
Or, as described in 1960, is de Kooning's *February*

"all sun, sky, earth, and sea"?
Februarius, fr. *februa,* pl. feast of purification
held on the 15th of this month; perh. akin to Gr.
thyein to burn sacrifice, L. *fumus* smoke, vapor

The act of painting as a februation,
the freedom to belly a grand,
to lay down an X-patch of light-red subliminal
rupture above an erection on stilts—
around an ape-attached-jaw-keyboard-rump
to splash a squarish, splinter-flecked
pool of darker red—not blood red—
dull red coursed by unreadable dark,

satiation magnetism, which,
    under the spell of purification,
                    projects a Luba head,
a Congo ghost   (and now I see both eyes
                              goat-like,   pleading

            adorned and bladed.

NOTES ON EXILE AND PARADISE

[for Bei Dao]

The castle may be locked,
but a side keep is always open for the octopodal friend
coiling along the night road with his tentacular
   load,   broken
      and loaded,
struggling with his beak,
sent out by the great mother to hunt.

•

All poets are *ronin* ("wave people"),
liuwang,   "wandering in escape"
we've lost our master and are glad—

we're trailing our leashes,
our leashes track what we've escaped.
We despise exile.
There is interior exile
or,   there is no poetry
without the severing of master accord.

•

Is the power of a god only revealed in exile?
Must one be away from the familiar
to feel the gaze of transpersonal creation?

   1963: I was standing at the stern
crossing the Japan Inland Sea,
shafts of sunlight pierced the cloud layer
"Jewel Spears of heaven,"

at their tips I began to churn,
I was on a pyramid with infinite steps
ascending descending through each,
intersecting escalators,
an axis of twinning

from which I was as suddenly
banished.

•

As one wanders close to the paradise one is always inventing,
one become "potent with orphanhood,"
pregnant with the nightside   "closeness" invents for itself.

•

Is it in exile,
and only in exile,
that we might cross the Abyss?
And what is it to *cross the Abyss*?
To experience the absence of soul
while hovering over one's non-existence?
To say "I do" to "I am not"?
To imagine absolute absence?
Horrah Pornoff Comics,
speaking out of non-existence,
voice that *is* non-existence.

•

Haunted by a desert I have never crossed

    At the anti-center
I cling, a disturbed
peach, peeling

instead of dropping

Roots are for trees, not for men,
the air is unclimbable
unless you have a mushroom cane.
Something happens here akin to origin.
I pass up under the Spider Queen's veil,
lift up her festering egg-sac smile
that the radiance behind her moth-stained tusks
might clarify my passage.
Or call it another pulled-inside-out story.
Skullracks flash up the goer's robe
ascential-descential sensation,
peristalsis of the plover
eating and excreting in mid-veer.

•

In exile
within language, thrusting toward the margin
pulling back,
Larry Eigner's typing aslide south-
east bound—there's an anti-inherency at work
within associational errancy,
caricature of exile:
Chaplin aloop the cogs, syntactical
log jam,
so birl.

•

Gods Demigods Humans Animals Yidags and
the Dead all in my
plate,
Shenje gripping the Wheel of Life,
the endangered and the extinct

in a Chinese-American restaurant,
exiled within exile,
        goal of all beings,
meat holding chopsticks probing meat.

•

Are the dead in exile?
Or are they enisled within the lake of our green
   lion heart,
clustered trillions
at the wall of our *cor duplex*?

A divided heart causes our circulation,
miming exile's impassable wall.

•

Walks-with-his-house-on-his-head met
Walks-with-his-cave-in-his-head

"I bear my own abyss,"
said the latter,

"Inside are urns of honey
watched over by

the beehive-lady of Willendorf."
And the former said:

"Pull your cave inside out
and you'll have my house

or my cathedral
over your cellar, my paradise

over your pit."
Then both exchanged eyes

that emptiness might see
and fulfillment become blind.

•

I look at a reproduction of Hiroshige's "Plum Garden, Kamata," and sense paradise. Nascent white plum blossoms dot a persimmon raw silk sky, over moss-green grass without depth or blade. It is not Whitman's grass. It is, relative to Whitman, inorganic, artificial (as the grass in paradise would have to be)—yet because of the shade, one feels change, but of such slowness that permanence almost holds. The actual and the visionary—not a churning visionary, more a delicate tilting of the actual toward the visionary—coincide, have lost seam, are in relaxed and radiant fusion.

On the open sleeping platform is a black and dark-blue futon, so I imagine that I am looking at night in paradise, which is neither black nor dark, as if the two tiny people standing before the azure lake in the far corner of the woodcut had gotten up in their sleep and strolled through an adagio of light dark green shadows under the sunless, starless, persimmon sky. The sense of well-being that Hiroshige offers me is so overwhelming that I realize: this paradise I am sensing is a distillation of my affirmative memory of years in Kyoto, a Kyoto to which I can never return. At the core of my Kyoto must be the discovery of my imagination. A period of extreme self-conflict, but shining through—as if kin to the shaded radiance I find in Hiroshige—was the sensation: I can't, but I can. I can work my can't . I can can't.

•

But do the ontological layers of the exile onion mean much to your gut despair, Bei Dao? And is your despair not umbilical to a vision of a place to which you may never be able to return? If you could return to China, you would not return to the place you envision having lost. Perhaps if you do return, you will suffer even more estrangement, because the paradox will be more intense there than it is in Davis, California (but that seems like such an American thought! born of a fractured ancientness; unlike you, I have little depth in my cemetery—when I seek out the deep American past, I can't get around the Indian Holocaust. So I shift to Europe, to the bottom of the *Inferno,* and notice that Satan is Upper Paleolithic man, the first reindeer-antlered "devil" up to his neck in ice, my ur-pagan ancestor, or Giant Form, my unmoving mover).

•

When I go to Europe for depth, am I not in exile to the possibility of depth at home? Indeed, where is home? In a media-transfixed planetary "global village," our constellations mix and link, suggesting that no place is without the spore of home. At the same time, our hearts will always be scored with the primal home, the locus of exile. The womb in imagination opens out into a realm of ancestors as, simultaneously, it bottlenecks our fate.

As we approach 2000, millennial Fundamentalism of every stripe proclaims that the earth has become flat again, that folds have been replaced by edges, and that at the edge of the one and only faith, the heretic drops into eternal torment.

When we look out the window, we may see grass and trees—we may also put on a TV set, like a post-modernist thinking cap, and experience the exile in mediated witnessing. Today, we are verging on the notion that there is no place that we do not see (in contrast to Rilke's earlier vision that there is no place that does not see us). While this seems true, media-wise, it also seems false. There are plenty of places you and I do not see, where media will not, or cannot, venture.

It is in university libraries that I have felt most exiled not from myself but from self, that synthesis always dangling before us, carrot of a paradise, as we move along, driven by our missing story, over ground that flashes: *no scene is ever reseen as such.* It is the "as such" that is exile's negative pole.

•

"Ah, all is vain in the winnowing of memory! all insane among the fifes of exile: the pure nautilus of free waters, the pure mover of our dreams ..."

HOUSE WARMING

Bei Dao's upturned, spectacled face
as he sings triumphantly,
over-voicing a young woman's passion,
intermingling her folksong
  as she sings of Mao?
  a departing lover?

Something Chinese deepens
exile to twinning,
a dyadic inscape of exile.
          Denied motherland,
Bei Dao latches on to her voice,
          vibrates there.
An almost extra-terrestrial smile sets forth,
    "on wings of song"
as if by voice alone
one could return

                  transcendence.

[Ann Arbor,
18 February 1994]

YACHATS, THE SHORE

Looking into littoral fog
the shore has always stopped me,
laid a barrier across association,
made writing by the sea
listless, as if stumbling about
an ode ... dangerous to stare
at nature and write—

•

Surf crests have leatherine
concaves
then it's all froth crawlers trill

Gigantic skirts with meandering hems,
slits in weave to sand

Little cliffs' white rubble,
high sizz then
"sundered parentage"

Ropes vertically aflow—
describe the sewing throwing:
Mumonkan stitch,   gateless
barrier

as if a text of iles
detextiled while
ile flexing
wound sound
perception stops,
a shushing weave whelms the eyes:
skyscrapers under nuclear barrage.

I'm a little boy in my glandbox
   sifting mommy purr,
the simmerunderoar   spreads
   a virus under tone
taking the lips back to suckle shapes,
   trom   bone
the slides of brass
      under 4:30 sun
silver   so glaucous pocked,
                                   more cicada
                              than constant

      Watch out for unity as you age,
   it's in cahoots with reduction

Be as these rocks not deluged,
just gleamy in their lenten instant

                              Myriad-glimmered
reason surfing the tectonics of dream,

Mallarmé's "throw" still tumbling in the air,

poetry as shipwreck,   oceanic page,
"a throw of the dice"   the gamble of alchemical research
"will never abolish chance"   no way
   to predetermine reception—

Unless a work of art is its own shipwreck
a master is proposed outside the maelstrom

Surf looks more perfect than I can imagine a god,
perfection that if not seen through
      dwarfs imagination—
seen through,   nature *is* imagination,
        roving tooth breast

on which I row
60 years a second

Pyramidal speed-ups
slow lozenges of satin steel
storied   pounce in rinse,
dipping sun drapes a mail
across the crestlets

then 7 gulls in muscular goodbye.

[28 May 1995]

LESS AND LESS WHOLLY ABSORBED, AWARE
of your resonance,   I am not simply my own conduits
but a focus of your and my flashing lights

Being porous enough to dynamite
one's own characteristics   is the gem
in the marriage
band of learning—this entwined opening out
makes sense of love,
that on this one trip (then nothing nothing forever
I choose to be with you daily,
inhaling,   holy,   our filings
mixed,   like birdsong
ter-weet cher-wee (Amazonian wood quail

What I delve is a multiplicity tinted
shaded, flavored   released
wound-erased
by your bright shafts

You have twinned my life,   doubled its spore

Never to forget
nor merely to remember:
I sit in a tow of language
mined, in clink with a mile-
stone rage for mortar
while a Tibetan
is forced to build with temple bricks
a latrine

OY

   from the clear bell of O
hang a y, make it droop a bit,
tie a tail to it, can't you already hear
a tin can banging the pavement?
Joy, sadness, and enthusiasm—
                    dead image in
   living image, which is which?
Compression of oy, dead fowl in motion,
twist of oy

"Once I saw the village butcher slice the neck of a bird and drain the blood out of it. I wanted to cry out, but his joyful expression caught the sound in my throat." Soutine patted his throat and continued: "This cry, I always feel it there. When, as a child, I drew a crude portrait of my teacher, I tried to rid myself of this cry, but in vain. When I painted the beef carcass it was this cry that I wanted to liberate. I still have not succeeded."

                    Oy caught in the throat,
making its midnight Noah journey through earth and flesh,
   Soutine's *terra convulsiva* is mole
in tar,   lit by a personal spectre,
   hungry, bulimic, and sincere,

or in looking at the hanging fowl,
Soutine is inside, claw twisting in a glove,
   is carcass home?
                         Unending regression to get back,
to be inside, not depict it,
hanged fowl   man hanged from his oy
   paradise as the prism of colors
radiating through funereal meats

To encave the delicious pheasant,
make it a tube in which mind,
    like peristaltic jelly, can inch

Insectile whirr of broken wings,
    resurrection—
                        unsure erection
hidden by the pastry chef's groin-centered
    knotted red towel
                            How empty O seems
afloat over Soutine,   how it hooks down,
into the off-stage, the obscene, into
    gristle bubbling with death

I still walk my eye-stalks through these gored
    and flowering fields,
stick insect pilgrim around the bend
beyond which Whitman no longer lingers—

                    art as snare, or
    mantis probing, copulatory
invasion, rifted by
    galactic wind.

IV

Soutine's Lapis

❐

in 1919, in Céret, where landscape
became unsayable outside
the sensation of up at 3 AM
easel strapped to back, trudging 20 km
to find the right spot
"Soutine on the road to Céret"
as Bacon painted "Van Gogh on the way to work"
horseheaded man bleeding into the firmament
ant-headed seer, roasting in
the eternal quest: how say this body?
how transfer this
unsayable power ladle gale beating
bedbug man?

So he spent all of Zborowski's
200 francs on paint, lived in a room with a pig,
and lived on handouts, no way to say it
landscape become gesture,
fractured leg of a road pick-up sticks
frontal assault of earth broiled orange
ghost facings caught in the husks of trunks

I'm looking at Soutine's Céret, the 60 surviving paintings
(he zealously destroyed 240,
hunting them down like animals, like the raven
he gave off at Céret, before being discovered by Barnes,
wealthy Dr. Barnes, who bulk-purchased at least
48 paintings, 1923,
the sale freaking Soutine's blind nerve—
he was to paint powerfully for another 5 years
by retreating into the 19th century
—is Barnes a bizarre version of Gachet? of Ferdière?
1923, Soutine's watershed,

he then revisits Rembrandt, Courbet, Corot,
    unaware that at Céret
he had contacted de Kooning, that at Céret
    his no way to say it
said no in a way that a new yes was said)

The exultation at Céret has the long dirty ghost legs
    of bony ravens,   it marches without body.
Terror is seminal. It says: I am not the spit
my father shined me with. All windows are monstrous eyes.
All houses pupiled caskets. I'm sorry but the road
    is in the sky,
I mean, the sky is pumping the road, I'm sorry
but the road is in pump with the sky, if you know what I lean.
A whole treed plaza picks up its sunderskirts and runs,
    ruby lava.
The earth is unsubstantial lapis
while his body is poised on a brush

You can't see what I see, reader,
so I have to mail you
red gristle howling away from black fire—
"Landscape with Gnarled Trees," yes,
but the sensation is tree-torrential hill-tides
binding houses buckling and elasticized

So many gorges, upon inspection,
have not scissor-faced mothers, but hammerhead fathers,
pockets of gold, of pus,   pockets of hearth and pomp
knotted in a wickerwork of forced labor, of freedom, of
    tearing burgeoning—
in Soutine's Céret, a quaked slob
discovers his mortitude, the chutes of his lying,
all the image leprosy percolating Smilovichi,
the beatings,   their energy,
being famished,   its energy,

the energy in being rejected,
the energy of *no*
romantic folklore

Clutchy belonging to something
inexistent until created. Think of it!
You have no life, painter,
until out of nothing you create it!
Out of nothing? Out of a village church
looking like a huge gold spider about to vomit.
Out of a trampled green hex.
But to paint the exploding raven head
in which sun and moon may be copulating,
to ball this gonadal wax into a honeycomb
then to invest it with one's own bees—

this is to travel,   this is to visit Soutine at Céret

Jigging farmhouses burnished by a urine-colored dusk,
scree on the move. Bovine
femurs inside of which villagers live.
The feel of noon at 3 AM. Dream of a deal
in which one's foetal cash register is clanged shut.
As for *should you be?* The argument at Céret
is a road upchucking a cascade of zilch.
As for *why?* White-haired butcher babbling tomatoes
in the swill of pink organs meaty flood of boils

O the primal slaughter before all the houses!
Garden of Blowsy Delights!
Slaughter so real it deflowers—
the barns are boozy with it!

And there is always a hill. Not a mountain,
nor a slope, nor a rise,
but something 100 times Soutine's height,

of porphyry,   of jasper,   lit within,
a bubbling town dump, shack-
faced urchins poking through what Spaniards
  sliced Indians into,
a shifty hill,   a shtetl,   a townlet,
morne on which Césaire's mother pedaled her Singer,
Dead Man's Drop where I sledded,
there is always a hill,   a peak,   an excel
from which we are falling,   a precipice
  of which we are the innards,

the traffic jam in paradise,
grid-lathered Babel,

to feel a potential versus life as you piss,
shipwrecked roofs,   this scowling thatch,
whitened oaks like goose necks
force-fed with nothing,   stretched forge
with corkscrew thighs,   sky-wired elms,
clap of a single cymbal,   sound of self-rounding,
fire of the stem called masturbation.
Turba Mass in male soul   we have yet to figure.
Men, those brutal bastards who never really
  get to be king of the hill.

❐

There is a deep road,
a lily lea,
a Tao
always opening, then sealed, within some part of us,
"this great wink of eternity,"
out of the chambered underground a yellow is snaking,
around park bench and tree,
a twinkling ripple,
more often than not bifurcating our would-be form

Cagnes-sur-mer houses rear back
exposing a mildewed apple-land,
the fairy tales Soutine had to have dreamed,
a pretty pig grabs his hand
—hey, wanta swim?
Hay-yellow male road,
berserk
among the elephant-trunk-swaying woods

In Blake's "The River of Life," women with infants swim a path-become-river flowing past idyllic trees and porticos, while others walk in the river playing flutes, and others gather from the river the clarified mana. An angel swoops low, pointing at the water as if to fertilize its glassy flow

Can destiny be worked out in scape?

I think Soutine at Cagnes lanced his Céret hump
to find a glistening Mediterranean wound,
a viaduct,
wild Kundalini,
vertical boa nosing heaven,
swollen boa,

undigested pigs and whippings still suffocating
  in its guts

Ark-like swing with which this road redetermines landscape,
the Tao of Soutine:
the La Gaude "variations,"
12 paintings,
the height of his joy,
childhood golem exulting,
hand up La Gaude making Porky Pig shapes out of houses,
a vine of godheads sprouts from the boa's side,
accordion village,
twists of whipped-cream courtship,
a detonation held in play,
too whipped through   to stay joy,
too avalanche,
too peak veering,
too dumped

    Caught in the act
the yellow boa road turns into red centipedal embarrassment,
all legs flattening and arching,
or is it a bloody spinal cord surfacing through wheat?
a way of being   extending clamps?
Now here come the houses!
They push their beer bellies up to the road,
bang it silly,
siphon off its undigested spunk

May Nile-turquoise manticores
speed thee to thy rest

"Church at Cagnes":
a just-marooned Atlantean
grasping his fate.

❐

The pheasant is risen.
The dead pheasant, risen from her bath—
out of tomatoes, she is risen,
the garrotted pheasant,   out of her vessel,
a still-life,   life in the still of
   alchemical imagination

It is very murky here, fleeced of sunlight.
The potted flowers grapple with the chair back.
The lilacs in their jug look like spoiled meat,
like scrapings turning scarlet with desire?
Jug acrawl with roses, looking Argus-eyed,
face swarming with eyes, roses as blowflies,
release these ravens, peacock entail them!

      and then some jonquil yellow
      some geranium
      a plaster statue
concerning which, the legend goes:
"embrace her with love, and deposit upon her some semen—
like Pygmalion's Galatea, this *fate* will come to life in your dreams
and tell you, now her lover, where to find buried treasure"

Song of the gladiola-spirit yearning for blood,
yearning to become what Soutine was unable to eat.
In the still-life retort, flowers feeling
   flow-er rapture,
a contra naturam, as Soutine nerves
flow through gladiolas,
                              Van Gogh is near,
the background blackens,   a putrefactio is under way.
Petals like copulating infants.
                    The canvas a urinal

in which the moon is lying on her back
                              in blackish water—
could we dissolve into this flower-flow,
what lurid wonders we'd unearth.
Soutine Van Gogh shaking hands in sperm,
squeezing pulpy red ocelots out of pressed palms,
flukes of childhood hunger resonating in the woods.
Scum of boiling, bloody broth, the fidgets, the blocks.
Resistance in the gladiola,   the word itself
unhinging, a "sword lily," diminutive of *gladius*.
Is the painter a gladiator? Little swords form a mandala,
a magic circle,   a fly is trapped under Soutine's eyelid.
He leaves it there. Fly rots, green cream forms over the eye.
The pot of flowers now looks like wilting antlers.
Van Gogh guffaws. How wring out these gladiolas?
He cuts his hand on the steel stalks,   forces them through
his mother's wringer,   *his mother's wringer,*
he looks out from between her legs, his mouth
stuffed with gladiola stems.   Self-Portrait as a Hydrant
Gushing Tulips.   A herring falls across.
He's still stuck in Smilovichi, plucked clean in Paris.
Van Gogh throws up into the pot. In the violet mess
   a storm begins to twinkle...

The herring's eye looks like a truffle floating in yolk

Explain the cephalopodic grasping of these tulips.
Explain
these manta talliths, this Cimmerican inkiness,
the way painted-over paintings (flea-market scrape-aways)
ouiji directions in circuit shock with Soutine's
once used, tossed away brushes

"I am the source of all pornography,"
sings the little flayed rabbit still in woolly socks,
"laid out on my pale gold and suet sheet,

my whole cavity is open to your eye-fingers,
    my legs are spread,
    my crotch smeared red,
    my wispy forelegs wiggle
    by my skinned but staring
    head"

According to Paracelsus, every body (meaning every tangible substance) is nothing but coagulated smoke breathing forth from the matter, or the matrix, in which it is present

Thus this pike "body," a sulphur fumet of cobalt, tar and
blood, slapped down on a shiny bench,
mouth rubble frozen in a paroxysm of snapping,
alongside a row of vermilion onions
which must be tomatoes,
little bloody turbans of smoke

Another pike-shaped flayed rabbit
so mutilated as it quivers in its violin
Bacon is immediately present,
or Bacon's grinder mind, through which this creature
seems to have passed

It has always given me pleasure simply to say Soutine's colors,
to reflect on the way his things interpenetrate,
a mahogany table whose cinnabar grain liquifies
around 4 steel-blue, grey and white fish
whose surging immobility is picked up by the rumpled, knotted
  ochre cloth

All here is living and dead at once,
as if half-frozen bodies were dropped on red-hot coals,
photographed in their first seizure,
glimpsed before the awakening became being awake

Some scholars have written that Soutine is dominated by anthropomorphic gestures, that he is undisciplined, hallucinated, out of control, a necrophile. To spot subliminal forces organizing in his limbo brawn is not to see him as cartoon-complexed; rather, it is to affirm the extent to which he turned the still-life into life in the still. Soutine is one of the most porous painters who ever lived. In the bloodmares to be found in the oily, night hair of his Seine are hybrid consequences still-dwelling in our minds-to-be-born

Such is his ray, a wealthy bawd, in the profusion of fat and jewels nosing forth out of the blackness of her latrine, while the pot of tomatoes below digests itself, tomatoes turning upon themselves, slipping up and around each other, anxious to burst

Or another ray, which appears to be disemboweling itself of tomatoes, parboiled and skinned, which Soutine cannot digest, a ray with multiple tomato breasts, O Ray of Ephesus!

Or still another ray scene in which a copper tea-kettle has come alive, flinging its ribbony handle-arms to the dark, dancing and leering at the 4 pomegranates inching toward it like seething little kegs of blood

The color and texture of this ray evokes the face of the older Rembrandt, jewel-like decay, mucous and cinders, creature as mineral, as flesh, as paint, in whose pocked and luminous surface a child is born and marked in Bethlehem

Annie Mae Grudger has been listening to all of this,
looking for many years now through Walker Evans' kind lens.
She is 27, has 4 children, wife of an Alabama cotton tenant
farmer,
and is nearly-starved. She is losing her hair,
holding her mouth in a smile-clench.
For a moment her humble bile has receded and she has offered
her tilted gaze to Evans' camera.

For a moment, she would walk out of her body
and embrace something she has just felt.
1936,   she is standing posed against
bare unpainted siding,
she is backed by Soutine

and it is her spirit that often shines in Soutine.
She is so thin at 27, you can see her upper chest bones,
she has one dress she could be photographed in,
no underwear, I'm guessing, nothing like a bra.
She might have some saggy, ripped panties.
Annie Mae Grudger is the Smilovichi intersect,
a cleaned-up version of Chaim locked by father
    in the chicken-coop

(I'd argue Barnes is the crucial provocation,
but clearly self-destruction is endemic to Soutine,
destruction of his self,   not himself,
destruction of what he made of himself,
Jewish hatred of the image,   bypassed by the man,
scorpion-tailing back on the painter,
he honors the terror of Smilovichi
when he slashes a Céret)

To be hanged in Venus-flail inside a crumbling chimney:
turkey in rotting turquoise high heels,
with sulphur Italian-blue henna Sapphire-blue breast,
aureoled in black, with circular buzz-saw of blue-black feathers.
To be at genital-lock with one's forge
lit up as if by interior bluebottles.
Ode to our wretched turning,   to be,
volatile body,   Soutine would deny Mercury
and insist that the body in glory
is the squirrel in the arbor
starved and pawing for chew.
Turkey carnal candy. Timid girl legs,

hesitating death-droopy talons.
Steatopygous chicken, whose larder lesions
purl with peppery gland streaks.
The Eden-rot of Maya. Texture of foggy morgue fuel.
Have you smelled a stale chicken? Have you,
Whitman might inquire, smelled your stale self?

"Yellow Turkey" with red flayed-rabbit-head
pointing lode-ward as if in pollinated
gyre,   carcass
already treacle,   moving with lice-accord.
This nothing we are,
arrested,   but not spent

And it is beautiful for things to get out of hand,
for the wine of Tartarus to soak through the snow,
for a turkey to hang and orange.
Corraled chaos inside of which a moldering
duck exults,   or is it a green eagle?

Turned on its side, the 1924
"Fowl Hanging Against Red Bricks"
becomes a chicken goddess propelling herself through an underwater grotto.
She has multiple breasts,   a human profile.
She is passing over a sunken red tugboat—
the disintegrating horizon of a subliminal Céret?

❒

Does Soutine, staring at a hanging rabbit, release some of his own fear of dying so as to fidget a ripple through the carcass he is conceiving? The part of Soutine brought to pause facing the actual animal flinches in the painting's image, a kind of reciprocity, a kind of molten exchange

Neck-broken roebuck. One hoof pinned to the canvas top center, another hoof dangling, a "limp wrist." The head sagging backward nuzzles what is identified as a "red curtain"—it is more like a down-jelling of blood. Swaying roebuck, pawing an abyss of chestnut green, nursing at Slaughterhouse Falls

Before confronting an entire beef carcass, Soutine painted sides of beef. The one in the Colin Collection evokes Bacon, then drives right through him. It *is* a side of beef, marbled violet, yellow, white, the top of which appears to be attached to a bin or trough, half of which is an odd linen-like white—and when I look again at the meat pressed into this "pillow," I see a screaming, flayed male head and, looking down, his body, belly pushed forward, ass jutting back, armless, the notched spinal column winding arm-like down, a reformulation of the centipedal sidewalks of Cagnes. The belly is so thrust forward, "pregnant" leaps to mind. In the inevitable comparison, Bacon's mutilated figures on beds are luscious, fleshy swirls. The Soutine is poised at the apex of the fusion of a sawed-in-half roebuck and a man flayed screaming on a bed

Pierre Courthion writes:

> Around 1925, Soutine tackled a series of gigantic pieces of meat. For the project, he rented a large studio flanked by a collapsing brick chimney on rue du Saint-Gothard, not far from the Denfert-Rochereau train station. In this workshop, which neighbors came to call "Soutine's Butchershop," he began to

paint, along with turkeys, cocks, and hanging ducks, enormous quarters of beef.

Paulette Jourdain, who was at this time Soutine's model and assistant, described to me the nearly unbreathable atmosphere of the workshop:

"I would pose," she said. "And watch the flies that came to tickle Soutine's nose. Then at the Villete slaughterhouse, he bought a whole beef that his dealer Zborowski paid 3500 francs for. Soutine was not aware that the beef would rot. I was sent to slaughterhouses to buy blood in a milk pail, blood which sprinkled on the blackening surface refreshed the so-called model. Downstairs, I would always run into the same characters questioning me: this blood, what is it for? For a sick person, I would say. O well, then, they'd exclaim, take care of him!

"Soutine would say to me: they gave you their most beautiful blood! How lucky I am to have you!

"When he was at work, he would throw himself from a distance *bang bang bang* at the canvas! I was made to stand behind it, and I was afraid. He bought used canvases, which he carefully scraped. He'd say: I like to paint on something smooth. I want my brush to *glide*.

"In that huge studio, I posed while the beef reposed. Big blue flies were circling about. These monsters are awful, Soutine would say, without noticing the putrefying stench to which he appeared to be accustomed.

"A knock at the door. Who's there?

"Sanitation Department!

"Panic. A uniformed man walked in to take the beef away. Soutine became deathly pale.

"O please, he begged, can't you see I'm working? I've got to finish my painting!

"Moved to pity, a worker in white came forward, and said to Soutine: watch what I'm going to do. He took out a syringe, a needle, and injected ammonia into the beef.

"The next day, the sanitation people came to disinfect the

studio. Soutine was able to continue. He completed the piece of beef on a blue ground that's in the Grenoble Museum.

"A day later, Soutine appeared with a bag of syringes. He furiously injected everything! The ducks became rigid as wood, although their feathers lost none of their color. End of the stench! But the carcasses we put out as garbage poisoned the neighborhood dogs. We ended up digging a hole and burying the ammonia-injected meat in quicklime."

In the life-spirit of pure blood
a lapis is dwelling. It is the whirlpool in chaos.
It kills, and it quickens.
Wonderful stone, held in derision by the world.
It is heaven. It is the scum of the sea.

The Buffalo "Carcass of Beef."
Threadlike black scribbles, drips,
antic milling in the pit of a colosseum
framed by the richest blue.
Tension at the top,   tolling
gravity below,   this glassy, roily fatalcore,
this animal crib become our slatherfest,
this sordid hackwhich, this Vietnam!
Stubblegrowth in loathed rubble,
the first god quaternified,
it is the animal garter soaked in us,
nigredo-overpowered alembic,
this predator temple,   this immense
Buddha-compassion breakdown,
   to disembowel,
to toss the liver to the wolves,
to core the animal of itself, and move in,
and once inside the animal house,
to start to work on oneself!

And then a mahogany-red pheasant comes twisting
through the waves of a semen-cream drape.

❐

Soutine's portraits are marvelous machines of consciousness.
The coils, the hairpin
turns, the tics,
muscle armor,
flabby troughs of that weighing station between
nothing and an enlarged suckling
each person is the patina of.
Crispate fingers that suggest the hand's desire to act
the octopus,
have a beak hidden in palm.
Hands knotted in prayer like an inflamed pumpkin.
Or glove-like, and melting,
fingers become nightcrawler independent,
hands as the exhausted straw of the body's peristalsis,
as in "Woman in Red,"
broken, paired slabs, stacked one on one.
There's a wildly-flopping turkey in each of us,
an atavistic flyer manacled to bipedal hesitation.
I like the whirling raw hamburger in his faces,
the drab fix of their stares.
"Village Idiot" and "Mad Woman" join
Madeleine Castaing in her black fur
and "Man with Straw Hat," whose face is toothpaste
being as squeezed impasto,
the epanadiplosis of the body
moiling back on its rhyme,
out of the shtetl, forever rocking,
a prayer metronome Whitman never knew...
repressed missions fade in the choir boy's eyes,
the white of his dress
almost redeems the color white,
it is as stained as an old cooking rag,
washed rewashed,

the flecks of parsley, garlic, rancid butter,
bits of chopped red pepper,
it is a tunic on which fowl have been dried,
in which parboiled tomatoes were squeezed into
little balls, to garnish
a chicken in champagne sauce.
The "Page Boy at Maxim's" blood-drenched-red uniform
breaks out on his face and hands,
or do his crimson ears and black eyebrow eye-pits
release their pained,
ruined, servile
clots into his uniform?
Soutine has drawn an empty circle on his outstretched palm,
the circle's slightly off,
the tip will never be right,
never connect with the need
beyond any tip
of one ground between tables,
whose life is errands.
These are faces as charged as marshes with their own
uroboric devouring,
heads whose source must be
in the privation of hewn and crafted images
from which Soutine's ancestors suffered.
The Biblical world sack turned inside out,
there tumbles forth
—along with flame-shaped praying men
and mousy pastry cooks with elephantine ears—
Soutine himself.

According to Maurice Sachs, he was "at first glance, coarse, unplaned, ill-shaped. A thick, haphazardly-planted nose, fleshy, pale lips opening on irregular teeth, a single thick eyebrow, stubborn and without malice, barring his forehead crowned with dense, black, tousled hair. His small, penetrating eyes were of a rare color, a kind of saturnine blue, and their speckled, mazarine grey irises were like fluid, lively, animated agates. He had short hands, but they were admirably shaped, agile and graceful."

Who *is* this "Woman in Pink"
we'd all like to know? She *is*
her coiling chair, a pythoness dredged,
battered, in moldy, foaming rose.

❐

1906. Maurice Tuchman writes: "Two of his older brothers constantly taunted him, saying 'A Jew does not paint.' They beat him mercilessly. This cruelty became almost a ritual. Soutine would flee his brothers and hide in the woods until hunger drove him home."

Amazing, given the Hitlerian shadow, to ponder his bundled, struggling-along children on French country roads in 1939. A boy holding the hand of his younger sister. Two boys sprawled on a log. Soutine in the woods at 46, still hiding from those who would watch him paint.

"One day, when Soutine was about sixteen, he approached a pious Jew and asked him to pose for a portrait. The next day the man's son and his friends thrashed Soutine viciously and left him for dead ... it was a week before he could walk again. A complaint was lodged against the aggressors by Soutine's mother, and the boy was granted as compensation the sum of twenty-five rubles.

With the money Soutine and Michel Kikoine set off for Minsk to become artists."

David Sylvester: "In the Céret paintings the forms are dense and congested and their nearness makes them loom up, dangerously close, threatening to burst through the picture-plane and having to be held at bay. As if fearing an attack from them, Soutine assaults them: the canvas becomes a battleground between the menacing force of whatever confronts the painter and the bending force of the painter's will.

"And this becomes Soutine's pattern—to put himself in a position from which he feels that something is threatening him, so that he must attack it, wrestle with it, twist it, wring its neck. It is as if he can only make contact with the external world through an act of violence and violation."

So the terrible beating that paid off, that brought him to Minsk, that enabled him to become a painter, is endlessly restaged, restated, nearly transformed. At some point in the late 1920s, the furnace of combat cools. As if to say, Soutine woke up one morning with the battle behind him, on the far side of transformation. As if the transformation were the moment of falling asleep, the moment we are always before, or beyond, never consciously *in*.

Such must be a captive freedom, a sort of horrible leisure (Bruckner counting tree leaves (Soutine spending hours looking for four-leaf clovers

By the early 1930s, Soutine appears to be travelling, as a painter, on a composite past. When he speaks of Rembrandt's "The Jewish Bride" (his favorite painting), he places his hand over his heart, mimicking the groom in the painting placing his hand over his bride's heart. Yet his "Woman Entering the Water," inspired by Rembrandt's "Hendrickje Bathing," is as coarse as Soutine himself. Painted in the rain, a peasant raises her soiled white dress, staring at thick, clubby legs—forbidden fruit?

His one "nude" holds her hands over her genitals, the hand on top reddening as it clutches, turning the wrist below it white—ashamed of her body, thoroughly ugly, her face seems to await a blow, or is it that she is already cuffed, jeered, called upon to perform like a dancing bear that cannot dance? She simply stands there, guilty of nothing, guilty of woman's body, tinged tawny in such a way that Nebuchadnezzar crawls by as I look at her, Blake's "creature" trapped between the human and the animal. Soutine's "nude" would be more aptly called "the naked one," or more fancifully "woman on the blackened chicken-run of her life," the pathetic source of his ancestral ambivalence toward image, the despised scapegoat cowering in what we call "sacred," our mother's body, its incestuous imprint on love's body, the gangrene usually hiding in the wings of the stage upon which the classical "nude" is unveiled.

A green chaos of magnificent trees sweeps through the last eight years of Soutine's life, soaring, waving poplars, oaks, beside roads outside Chartres, Civry, and Champigny. Trees like giant whisks tremor in awe of earth's arborescent flavor. For the first and only time in Soutine, one looks up into green dragons devouring blue serpents, a darkening stir, the caldron not on earth, but at cathedral tower level, where our eyes give out, where we peak, as watchers.

The engorged boa roads of Cagnes are now delta-shaped inlets, humble rural paths, the tiny children almost lost in ruts and greenery, lady bugs in the tapenade of the ground. The minuteness of the human relative to the vastness of nature recalls the Chinese floating world of sages perched on pine-covered, mist-swarmed cliffs.

Two children move along the road, as if biunes, strange twins, or little comrades with two arms gesturing from a single, fused body bearing two heads. These kids are Soutine with his natal daemon exulting in the grand and wrestling doorway of nature's slapstick vagina. The tininess of the children—really one child—and the overarching boiling breeze become Soutine's farewell. On a wander-route with his infant daemon, he is haloing himself back through and into the forestral gradations of the teepee-like entrance/exit all waver between.

In some of these paintings, the road seems to shoot through the little figures, and whirl on up between the trees to become a sky road. In others, the sky is like mucilage between the trees, an opaque "negative" of a ghost, not empty space but a sky-like non-sky

wind as porous disturbance   pointillistically dispersing the coagulated smoke that was life

ON A PHOTOGRAPH OF GALL

A mountainous shadow rains in stasis,
the extinction of indigenous person,
Gall,
the orphan adopted by Sitting Bull,
posed by Brady in regalia.
The defeat of Custer uncocked the Protestant arsenal—
Gall bears the weight of the pregnancy of extinction.
Dickinson's "a certain slant of light"
ricochets
"a pyramid of granite night."

EL MOZOTE

Lieutenant Colonel Domingo Monterrosa,
a   blown-apart girl wants to talk with you,
she wants to rearrange,   like checkers,
   a topological map of Morazan—
she wants to play, Lieutenant Colonel,
against your American power,
                                                she wants to see
if slit baby throats, raped beheaded girls,
can jump your American M-16s, 82 million dollars,
Lieutenant Colonel Domingo Monterrosa,
a disintegrated rib-cage wants to confront you
with her trinkets and little pencil,
                                    she wants to ask about
her friend who once had a bright-orange
plastic horse,   she wants to know
if the dug-up toy is the soul of her friend,
she wants to know if there is a soul,
Lieutenant Colonel,   she does not know,
Domingo Monterrosa, that the goodness of being
must include articulate responses to
bones sticking through rotting trousers,
that even through the most abstract Pollock,
                the most unglossable Zukofsky,
an American flag of smoke ripples
   in sublimNational honor
and in gallery, in book, our hearts die
for we know,   Lieutenant Monterrosa,
no matter how many of you are blown out of the sky,
the military killer factories we finance
                                are at work below

O unnamed girl who could have been
Rufina Amaya Marquez's daughter,

Rufina Amaya Marquez, who watched her four children
   and her husband slaughtered,
Rufina Amaya Marquez discovered
         days later cowering in a ravine,
naked, bloodsmeared, covered with thorns,
Rufina Amaya Marquez, El Mozote's only witness!

OUT TO SHOW THEM

"What is laid upon us is to accomplish the negative; the positive is already given."

If the horror swings by outside the poem's frame, do we say the frame is too small?

How be as vitally full as the negation surrounding me?

Danniel Hamm "had to, like, open the bruise up and let some bruise blood come out to show them."

Adopting a pelvic gaze, Hans Bellmer saw lingual oysters roving in a sole. Vixen-flecked femur filings. Pulling open the belly brickwork, he inspected the fecal sturgeons. Inside a scrotal pile-up he came upon The Holy Crater.

I took a draught of zero. It blew away my tears. My eyes rolled forward into dice space, knowing molecular surrounding cold.

"Paul Valéry's response to the final disease—'Je suis foutu et je m'en fous—I'm damned and I don't give a damn'—remains the best possible (even a religious spirit can find it exemplary). To be perfectly wise without ceasing to be human, pronounce the first part firmly (realization of the ineluctable fact: 'Je suis foutu!' Good! You're right!) and the second part with secret reluctance, a slight hesitation, to spare one's reality from trembling at the prospect of a loss one fears complete—that of everything the unsaved person believes himself or herself to be. On close reflection, Valéry's response also suits nations, empires, religions, civilizations, and the whole of mankind—every apparition of matter."

Damned to give a damn ...

AT XOCHICALCO

—a ball court stone hoop
half-embedded in the ground.
A geometric spider web spans the arc.
That spider, hanging there,
shovels a faceful of caresses into me,
caresses of a Chiapas child, full of worms and lice,
   trying to read,
caresses of: to win is to live what it is to lose,
caresses of "Woman, your body is the battlefield!"
caresses of the line cut by Adam's black diamond in the glass
   of virginity,
caresses of the player-thudding ball court of the dead,
can absolute absence be said?

Absolute division between the living and the dead

Poetry to span the absolute,
hovering over,   baby spider cast into the breeze,
to report what it sees below:
the moisture on the pyromaniac's skin,
Neruda getting Trotsky's assassin out of Coyoacan,
the potty of a saint,
chess pieces slippery with blood,
a spider the size of a field mouse digesting a hummingbird
   while it whirrs.

ALL THE ONLY ONE

The anguish of giving birth to warriors,
or baby girls
to be set down in the male wilderness and,
like young rabbits, effectively abandoned

breath of rust
breath of blood-on-the-cob

the way a man can open up
and then be gulped down whole by
another man's greater need

the Eden a geek is made to ape
gnawing snake
in her round chain-linked pen

far from the carnival's glassy core

shimmers we use like fans to disguise our fangs.

PIT BULL LOOPED TO CATHEDRAL IRONWORK
—eyes deftly cored ruby.
Beast profile as petrified semen

Inside the cafe across the street,
on TV: Holyfield's back,
a great shield, muscles cogging,
a ringside window on the utterly moving
emptiness of being.

LIBERATION FOOTAGE

Naked corpses dragged and dumped
into pits of 5000 by Belsen SS guards
under US surveillance, April 1945,
limber as hammocks
unresistant
deep long white valleys
where stomachs had been,
or bodies bumping along, muscle free,
deep long white valleys
hoisted flopping onto SS shoulders,
they hated it they had to do it they
heaved them up from Belsen trucks
spread-eagled, trash they hauled

By the green
slaughterhouse within
my lawnmower,

a naked
child offers honey to
a wingless bee

There is no proposal the imagination cannot assimilate

But it is only through Pleistocene mercy that we're still here.

GRETNA GREEN

I saw the Beast
an octopoid cephalopod, bat-winged and clawed in its lower extremities, possessed of a central glowing eye—reddish and baleful—set at the top of its head. In the lower part of the face (where I anticipated a mouth) was a mass of writhing tentacles, eight in number

I saw a second animal
a disemboweled half-skinned horse-sized white wolf bitch lying on her side in a pool of half-melted snow, the red of the blood spreading

the dragon tree overhead bloomed inflamed pulp

I saw a third figure
a rigid ash-faced fetish whose scalp, neck, chest, abdomen and thighs bristled with knives, inset mirrors, and nails. Out of its O-scream a fish-line hung with five rubies of blood encircled the wolf and disappeared into the Beast's glowing eye

I pegged it as the American Abyss within the Beast, in whose historical depth of night and fog I now saw lynched blacks like noosed dry-cleaning shuttling around and around the courtroom

Immobile as an Easter Island god, listening to his lawyers' arguments, the Beast is humanized by a mediating language. The courtroom drama cocoons, enveloping the crime, as by chart and testimony it layers a teratomatous pupa composed of the Beast, the disemboweled wolf, and the Nkonde-Brentwood fetish

Could this pupa split its chrysalis, what would we see? White youths holding up crisply-cooked livers and toes, asking for bids? Or would a revelation of *the soul of murder* suck us through time back to a savannah to be devoured and divided between saber-tooth energy and excrement, and discharged with the absolute force by which man woman and serpent were expelled from Paradise?

Every culture has a human sacrifice hidden in its invisible foundations. Ours is an Indian woman masked as Aunt Jemima scrubbing the condominium walkway

Then I heard a voice whisper to the Beast:
"you an'me, baby, we're like two foetuses
in the belly of that dead white bitch,
no way we're going to get out
—but we did!"

I, FRIEDRICH SCHRÖDER-SONNENSTERN
must confess that while I am male
I am prognathous and female, with queenly tresses
triculating my loins. A lovebird
pecks at my butt notch. Nipple-tripodal,
I salute at attention my red rooster king
who, at serpentine attention against me,
gives me a clitoral nudge—
deft, sensational! while squirting in
a blue petunia
without losing hold of his switch!

My king, who is my confrontational
aplomb, is as stationary as I. We are engaged!
without engagement. His paSSion is displayed
through the life in his butt—
that's where the rainbow begins.
On his bright-red butt plate
there's Mr. Mouse with his millepedal tail!

I stand before you, arms outstretched,
in a long white robe, THE SANDWICH KING.
Why not? Jesus fed the multitude!
My cognac beard trails back to Aesop.
I raised my hyena clit to challenge Zeus!

It's great fun to be the visible inside of an outside
others take to be opaque.
The concentration required
is a spectre licking my anal razors

Man is a moon-moral
ass-driver who, with hidden raised switch,

offers a thermometer, disguised as a baby-bottle,
to the kneeling ass.
There are clearly too many smiles snaking up our hatred,
too many scimitar grins,
as the animal prays, broken-legged, before us,
nipple-suctioned to our own desire

Then, a second wind: a headless woman met me upside down.
Poised in the pubic
slot of her great buttocky heart: an erect eye!
I named her Moral Practice, and for her alone
learned deep muff diving,
the most mooned of the erotic arts!

Like most visions, mine is giddy, fractal—
you can't overdo an undone thing!
Who knows why I'm a glee-frozen Noah
displaying my ark like an unzipped whale?
I am Mystery Man not in fedora but in tux,
with Christmas tree limbs radiating out.
I am Moishe Kapoyr with finger wisps,
my nose arabesqued with helpless furls. Yet I am likewise
a version of the Gorgon few if any recognize

Not feet, but wheels—so the Devil can roll us about!
The Devil, he does not smile—O but he does,
oh but his big butt! the Devil's ass is rich, and red,
ooh tomato! The sword-toothed fat-boobed
vulture carrying away your angelic daughter
is the dentata inside my plot!

What I love is bulbous:
canaries bussing on my fontanelle.
What I love is armless:
Adam and Eve's passion for truth, as,
swung up through their legs, they stare at

their own butts!

All are on a boat, rainbow-energied.
All are ghoul-chewed by the moon. Man is
the ass turbined masterblend
of the moon—and there are no moral clues:
across my team of twelve plowgirls, I, my mother,
crack my whip! There has never been a Fritzclown
braincrown like mine! Propose—
and Psyche differs, and in her duff
a vaginal circumflex glows.
O emphasize the natal clitosphere in which
I, Friedrich Schröder-Sonnenstern, am actual!
Swans in udder gowns with rainbow hoofs testify:
there is way too much twat serum
for the fragile angel complex! and so I cut
to another scene, and passed out fishburgers, and who
will worship me?

In an assfield of corn, a brain is mourning

What I perform is gorgeous, and absolutely aligned.
At center: a smile stud.
Below: Piscean eye ambiguity.
A rump with spread and planted skull feet
is in position
                    O let your long turd drop!
There is no chamber pot without a heart!
And your turd, despite its andouille handsomeness,
will never reach its gloppingplace—
for your turd is not your own!

World, are you ready to travel?

Sod, have you finally sprung a man?

As a moonbeam trying to shoot an arrow
into the distant labyrinth of a sparrow,
I am sure. The toy master feeds the lion
boobe-myseh, while the toy ape toots.
Paradise is to change the sex of another's face
into a larval diadem of flames and lace!
So with knockers proud as zeppelins,
a toy propeller out my butt,
silk garters on each ham
and Pandora's tongue-shaped foot,
I am the conductor of my own Pandemonium,
a weight-lifter spider in a fly-infested tomb!

VI

My Evening with Artaud & Othlor

❐

While I never met Antonin Artaud, I did witness his performance, while in the wings, at the Vieux-Colombier, in Paris, 1947. I was eleven, and after a decision that collided with all her past behavior, my mother laid in a sizeable supply of salami for my father, buttoned him in bed, and we took off, two naïfs from Indianapolis, to bear witness to what my mother's choir master promised would be
the overturning of the cross,

or,

the planted body sprouting
through the bulb of its own barrier.

We slipped into the hall, stubs in hand, past Gide, Paulhan, Marthe Robert, a young Paule Thévenin, and others I have come to know through the lexical corpses littering the writing of my second magician (Blackstone, at the Circle Theatre the year before, being my first). Shortly after our complicated return, my mother completed the trinity of my early initiations by taking me to see *Tarzan's Desert Mystery*, my introduction to caves and spiders.

What moved me so much about my mother's behavior:
she did not yet know that I was born!
How close we were in those days!

While Artaud stripped, I thought of my sex life with my mother. The most moving months had been inside her, and while there were gaps in my foetal memory, what happened there, as I gesticulated to her every thrust, recalled my own closed-eye vision which I began to practice at eight. Pressing my knuckles into my closed eyelids, I manufactured stars, lagoons, lace stockings, blasted cities and kaleidoscopic diamonds which, watching Artaud, struck me as arterial beholdings, or seeings into my own seams which were, in effect, those of my my mother.

The fact that we merge into the egg, as a zero or gleam, to then remain bouncifully suspended there in a solitary confinement that is the least solitary we will come to know—this seems to suggest something about the unhappiness of men, who emerge hypnotised by an infolding warmth for which they will search throughout their lives but never rediscover—not in philosophy, nor in bathing.

Women while pregnant return to the womb, in men's eyes, and even if never pregnant, appreciate a "summer's full" in a way that men brood about or rapinely chafe against. Womb life, that vague memory of being coated with a pond that goes out into infinity, this memory, bachelored by the awareness that it almost certainly cannot be recontacted, this drives men to fury! We suppose dogs do not see their death, but that men do, without the certainty that it is final or the mitigation of a new life starting up inside.

Sitting by my mother, as she kept squeezing my hand, reminding me of a frightened female mole pursued by an aroused male, and watching Artaud divest himself of everything—this sitting by one who would burrow into me, while watching this foetal dance, man in the glade of himself, a kind of pinhead deprived of sunlight—my thoughts desubordinated fugally.

It was amazing to be by the one who made me, who took another's gleam seriously, while watching, right before my eyes, what life had in store for me. Artaud's bat-like reclutching, the way his "mutual aid" clothes failed to fit (though seemed, like a tree after a storm, perfectly right), his acrobatic introspections speared in mid-flight, the lullaby always about to emerge that, upon croon, swerved into loon-like wailing, then shot straight up to golden-shower the crowd while, at the same time, he was more arachnoid than anyone, more packed with eaten heads, more guilty—

this display made me feel that Artaud had at long last gone beyond his stymied Theatre of Cruelty, that this evening we were witness to the first performance of

an Amniotic Theater.

Artaud's complaint seemed to palpitate a disappearance. And it was: man reaches a limit of contraction at birth from which he seldom recovers. I whispered this to Gladys as she dug at my palm and, card that she was, she whispered back:

"Why you old fox! Go on, go on!"

Man is in contraction at birth because not only the essential, but the armature of the essential, and its ruthless anatomical aftermath, have been determined. At birth, man's invisibility is greater than his visibility, for he has been stiffed of eternity by those two sphinxes who made his manifestation possible. Some find profundity in the egg. Artaud was appalled by it. He once wrote that "the EGG state is the anti-Artaud state *par excellence.*"

It seemed that we stayed in these wings for many years. It seems that Artaud, ravaged and enraged, hands flying like birds around his face, declaimed his scarcely-audible poems throughout my adolescence, and that during this period I remained in the wings, watching the poet, then the audience, motionless by my mother, who occupied herself with needlework, occasionally asking me to play "White Christmas," "Rustle of Spring," or Chopin's "Revolutionary Etude."

Artaud would strip down to nothing, lose his skeleton in a wild flurry of looking, become two sockets bouncing about the stage, then joint by joint reappear, throw on his black rags, grab his manuscripts, and start to howl again.

Bud Powell visited, as did Lennie Tristano. The audience left, then returned, the auditorium filled with snow, sand blew in from Morocco. What are we doing here, I would ask mother.

Then she would hand me the Bible that Reverend Ragan had inscribed to me. As if suddenly plunged back into an asylum, Artaud would stop, twitch, and glare. His consternation told me that I must create my own Bible or be enslaved by another man's.

In a pale imitation of the soul, I would get dressed, first slipping on my pajama pants, then my wool suit pants. This way I wouldn't scratch so much in the pew that I would disturb the trances of those nearby.

In a pale imitation of the soul. All seemed to seem, even Artaud, even when he grabbed his crotch while cartwheeling around it, yelling that mommy-daddy was the monstrous absence in presence.

The monstrous absence in presence, a fugal occlusion, the dead fish in hand feeling of one's most treasured erection. The way life winks through every rigid expression. One seeks a rudder in all of this, a broom handle bobbling in the whirlpool, anything that smacks of being moored. Moored to what? Mother's smile?

"The basis of pornography," my mother leaned over to me, "is the impersonality of generation."

Artaud was taking a break, and Gide, who had fluttered to the ceiling of the Vieux-Colombier, had just descended, billing and cooing about Antonin's shoulders.

"Frankly, I'm appalled by it," she continued, "but I had to realize that my Chicago choirmaster, who came on to me before you, had a keener contour than daddy did that night in 1934, Philadelphia to be exact, when he slid into me as if I had walked into a hurricane. I buried my feelings in an entry in my Wannamaker Diary, commenting on a car accident, but you, my sweet sailor, became the curl of that lunge, and in many ways you are as personal as impersonal."

You are very naughty, I told mother—such information is beneath pornography, which was revolutionary in 18th century France, but today it's not even the cleavage you just displayed.

"Listen," mother dug, "solidarity is our only hope. There are midnights as pristine as Keats' nightingale, and others so jagged only a Shakespeare could bevel them. Cock in cunt, pardon me, my son, is celebrated not only in the English copula but is rampant in the metaphorical underworld. It is our lie, our magnificent nonsense. Humankind can only stand so much fucking. We Hoosiers understand T. S. Eliot's wisdom thus: piston in groove, oiled in and out, ongoing, for thirty minutes, to funeral parlor fusion, is simply too close to the void that, as your mother, I have brought you here to witness. And it is the void that terrifies us Christians, for we have no place to put it, no tequila and marigold bridge by which to cross the cross. The crucified is obviously stuck there and unable to assist. If Mary Magdalene were truly Magdalenian, surely she would have dragged him, cross and all, into the cave and succored him. And if they crucify me for our conversation—"

(mother turned to me like a dead, drowned dog)

"—would you roll away the rock?"

Frankly, I was furiously scribbling, and had almost tabled my dear mother's plea. Gide and Artaud were entwined on the dais, the audience was out smoking and quaffing. As a mortified eleven-year-old, I decided it was time to confront eating pussy. Simply having been down there, between Vala's legs, peering up across her tummy and crossed eyes, had offered me a brief but untutored perspective on male and female relationships. I had felt subordinate for the first time—and indeed, wife I was to Vala's barely-haired timid slit. We had been in the rumbleseat of paradise, a May Saturday afternoon, the orchestra of hell thrumming through our mettle. It's V for me, I recalled murmuring, lick to jolt.

Mother saw the blaze in my furrow, held a match to me, then lit up, incandescent.

"I could never get daddy to pray. I aligned him, perfumed my nest, even set up a mirror system by which, were he to roll over, he could reflect on the nature of the void. Prayer as cunnilingus, humbling and potent—only a maven could find a beat in it capable of tripping his own heart's arrogance. The man who scarfs his lunch from the trough of the goddess—this is the way we used to put it in Wabash—is injured in the act; he will never replay the hero, and who, dear son, is a hero after Odysseus? Men adore sexual mobility, parading full orchestras across the body of one passive, but to face this fateful gate, this Song of Songs, is to know the pump runs dry, and that the sacred is as much a scab as a mountain."

"I love to be broken down into the conversation we are having," mother continued. "If Antonin and André could fully explore, I'd like to think they would happily include the character of each as well as the void. This is where the lower body comes in, as a teaching device. The upper body, that palace of enforced certainty, is a battered though beloved icon. I love you most totally thinking of you as a cigar boy, just a torso and saucy head, no inquiring hands. If I had my way, I'd keep you like a jumping bean on the fireplace mantle forever. But since we are all products of each other's imaginations, I am quite aware of your serpent tail—such will not get you a MacArthur, but because you scuttle where you bleed, there are those in the future who will think of you, momentarily, as they pray..."

Her voice seemed to trail. Artaud was back, Gide in the audience. A poisoned stillness reigned. I realized that Artaud had not lived as he felt he should live until he died in electroshock, and that the first half of his writing life had been one long complaint that he was dead—

then the beauty and the dreadfulness of the poetic act broke across me. All poets, I premised, seek to be born in their work, and if we take that nothing backwards, then one begins as a deadman, and the deadman, even if regeneration occurs, is always there, a mummy or mommy-mummer, in the crease of realization. So that the poet is dead to but alive for a mouthless speaking, through which death, voiced, enlivens us. The poet is the dale through which countless copulations have passed, a sorghum of matted bee deaths, in hive to a flowering only those who suck at the source feel like hooraying. And then it struck me that everything I had just said could be stood on its head, because if one thing is true about life, its opposite is also true. Yes, the poet is the one who sucks at the vulvic, penile, or anal source, but the poet is also the one who refuses, and enaltars the consummation. Then a beautiful light spoke: Bodhisattva, stay with the peak.

Artaud was back in zoom, I felt like a flit, and mother? Tired as we all were, she moved on, slipping into the prompter box before Artaud's feet.

It was in this box, that in 1970, I buried her vertically. I was thirty-five, and have had many years to reflect on our fantastic evening at Vieux-Colombier.

❐

"Concerning your jumping bean status," my mother continued
—listen, I said, you are not my mother,
you are the interior mommy who ages as the speaker,
a figure called mutha,   or mutho,   or othlor,
a lobbying for terrain in my early adolescence
"—you listen," Gladys spat,
"I didn't holeschool you on Artaud for limbo!
Don't you see, Clayton Junior, we have you coming and going,
you were of me—bounced out,   there I was again.
Male life is confined to square one,
call it a keep or square it with Jung.
It is time we laid out your savior here,
time that you put your savior on..."

This kind of conversation with one's mom puts jism into Jesus,
it weights poetry's resurrection—
give Jesus some jism so he can spurt off the cross,
recon his image, remember him as virile and ordered,
capable of error, think of him as an army dog
who saves wounded soldiers, the real hero of your Sunday
School fantasies...

None of this was planned, not a word set in forecast,
all of it, one calligraphic stroke—
but last night, at fifty-nine, and at 4 AM,
I woke to an ending that the boy of eleven could not
have caught:
the stage of the Vieux-Colombier shifting fog,
the curtains crumbling, billowing grit,
and the audience? looked like Emily's gazing grain.
I saw goal posts outside the Rodez asylum,
felt the excrement in excrescence,
the extent to which incarnation is incarceration,
then I saw the white recluse

hammering out her diadem,
the infantile and the anile
in placental clasp—

Poetry in attempting to go beyond itself
nearly always reties its elf to a lumbering coffin mouse,
not that the circle comes full (choking
on its plenum),
but that foetal eyes peep from funeral bouquets.
Facing a plan (really, a vision as to how
to end this poem),
I understood the charge of poetry is to be alert
over and under the whorl, to contact the shark
and travel as its pilot.

Now I saw Artaud as a brown recluse flexing on a hammock,
masturbating sperm into its catch,
then with boxing-glove paps
inducting the sperm, as one might fill a fountain-pen.
Loaded, the Artaud recluse went off to seek his othlor.
"I do not want to eat my poem,
but I want to give my heart to my poem"
—not bad for one under electroshock in 1944 Europe.

My task is to imagine Artaud's
ascent,
drawing up his lower body into a leggy packet,
so that his toothless, fang-shaped head is surrounded
only by legs—his walking tree of will, without organs—
an eight-legged head bearing its sperm-swollen paps.

The Artaud Recluse, bearing boxing-glove masses of sperm
up into The Milky Othlor,   crawling the Great Rift,
passing over the Coalsack of the Crux,
thrumming on the Ophelia vent,   pushing into the caul,
retrieving his foetus,   burning his foetal toxin,
pummeling self-purged semen into sidereal Sunyata.

VII

THE ATMOSPHERE, LES EYZIES

Lazy pin-ball machine of bird sound balls
scoring the paradise
effluvia swarming my ankles

Bird-coded lay of breeze, of an everywhere nourishing
 latency

A single smoking road runs from Indianapolis to Lascaux!

A car storms down the road mush of tire lore

The lees in the air, gnat-fossiled
dead fresh stone at cut with thrasher folly,
congruent to
the nothing-saturated weir of
 air as
 vascular cenotaph

Night here is porcelain, plover, flail of a distant
 vanishment

The Vézère Valley a noctaduct
channeling the presence of 50,000 years

 Sound studs
in the grip of percolator wood cores

The smell of the infinite:
persimmon smashed limestone in helium dress

Freshness rowing alphabetically through stone
as a nonsense articulating *aurochs*—

the soul of its omenhood, a word now without animal

adust with the fortitude of pollen

Let me set terror back into the grass, inject it
deeply into the planet's skin,
get *chasm* back into *abyss*

        All nipples are Ivory Towers
    about which Unknowingness
                                        drinks.

[Hotel Cro-Magnon,
1 June 1987]

ABRI DU CRO-MAGNON WAS EARLIER ABRI DU
Cramagnon, emphasizing the *craw*
of the site,
craw and "cro" combined: belly hole in which 4 adult skulls and the ribs of a 10 week old were discovered under hearth remains—containing cave bear, cave lion, mammoth, spermophile, reindeer, horse, and possibly arctic fox bones—in yellowish clayey earth at Level I, in 1868. Skulls B, C, and D were of 30 year olds (two men, one woman); skull A was that of a 50 year old man, with "peculiar eroded patches on his bones, including a saucer-shaped depression on his right forehead ... related to a fungal infection called actinomycosis, which attacked [him] in his jaw area, and is known to have fatal consequences if it becomes localized in the intestines. One can readily imagine the alarm and superstition that must have attended the onset of each disease. Perhaps intricate herbal remedies were tried ..."

"The skull is markedly low in relation to its length. Long skulls are usually accompanied by narrow faces, but the facial skeleton of the Cromagnids is 'disharmonic,' for it is very wide. This 'disharmony' is one of the most distinctive features of the Cromagnids."

The limestone hill containing the shelter, crowned by a mushroom-shaped rock, serves as the back wall for Hotel Cro-Magnon.
Today the shelter is swept clean,
much of its overhang gone,
it is protected by a low stone wall, iron fence
and little gate, allowing me to enter
this *temenos* and pace, brooding on
chronic belatedness. The party's over! Does only
the empty beer can of this site remain?
Abri du Cro-Magnon, a kind of lower mouth, toothless,
the jaw silted (Levels A–J) to the epiglottis level,

I walk the tongue of metaphor
as off a pirate plank into 20th century Dordogne light,
thistly bird twitters, and an elderly American who inquires:
"Is this where they discovered man?"
I feel the extent to which I'm storied,
but the stories are under (first trace of fire: Level B),
pebble histories, midden chapters,
"Payroll of Bones" indeed!
The dead line up to collect their atmospheric wages,
I stand among them, a mauve ghost,
last night's supper a pouch of nutriment
their sockets search as they assemble
clacking and coming back into sound as this gruel
engravels them: *god wot cud lor* I hear,
cord loot mor torn,   sutra march of thing sounds,
at Level I something is still active–
is this the limbic pun-crawled division into which
20th century poetry suspends itself?
"Speak for yourself"   the necessary, baleful command.
Faced with so much story, I release my grip
from Whitman's hand,   "agonies are one of my changes of
    garments"–in the face of Auschwitz?
"I am the man.... I suffered.... I was there...."
The voice coalescing *Leaves of Grass* is still
convinced of perpetuity,   the grass will grow
forever from the skulls of white-haired mothers
regardless the Civil War pyramids of amputated limbs.
As Lascaux "emerges" in 1940,
Belsen begins to smoke on nearly the same horizon.
Then Dresden, Hiroshima ...   "We would have lost one
million boys had we attempted a land invasion of Japan"
–whose voice? of what species of compassion?
(surely not Whitman's)   A voice that no longer
believes in martial brotherhood (for Whitman,
arm-locked gore is one of the fraternal changes)
It is the nuclear mind, addressing us from a cloud!

"Century O century of clouds"
Century of Black Holes

Abri du Cro-Magnon
Big Hole Shelter

—come of chronically-belated age at last,
I translate as: Big Hole Man.

NEANDERTAL SKULL

Flared sockets under
bulging brow ridges tough as tusks
evoke rock shelters with visible rear walls.
In countermotion to cheekbones sweeping back,
incisors—carrot-orange at base,
surfaces warped from gripping hide—buck forward,
a third arm,
an anatomical vise.
As if this convex brow glacially furled the cranium back,
flattening it,
lifting facial planes toward mid-morning sun.

Our smaller faces are tucked
in, beneath our brain-case's dome.
Rectangular sockets tilting outwardly down
imply our brow beam is bending under awesome pull.
Our sockets aim straight into auroral red,
their cranial pits evoke deep caves,
sealed hidden wealth,
mind a synesthetic abyss.

Weregaze oriented to "the wild, blue yonder,"
did Neandertal have an interior
refuge in which to refoetalize and fantasize a bow?
Scavenging in dread,
under predator arrest,
Neandertal took the Paleolithic's full assault.

La Ferrassie

PLEROMA

Chestnut   linden   aflutter
   sudden rain-promising gust
downshift of light,
            breeze streaming through both
wall-length doors,
                              wind, earliest
inseminator,   the pyramid left open to the west,
            let the dead Queen circulate,
      Iris,   available to all,
   birthing Eros,   Iriseros,
                              perichoresis

Now the trickle   asphalt perfume rising

Then as quickly   light returns,
a patter sifts the pour—

        The cliffs of Les Eyzies erupt
and hold,   as if this were the green
    navel of the Abyss,   wild cherry
                              thistle
                              dandelion
                              wild artichoke
                              hellbore
                              birch
                              oak
                              chestnut
                              fennel
                              asphodel &
                              juniper are the ancient
                              flora

The linden over the terrace is a shimmering

bushel of green, taking the 6 PM light
  on raised whitened leaf undersides

Over the candle-flowering chestnuts,   over
Hotel Cro-Magnon,
                    a bulging, ribbed, Cretaceous
        limestone forethinker,
                              the oolitic

                Promethea.

BARCAROLE

This evening the sky over Les Eyzies:
lead-blue, enamel-blue, azure, baby-blue, milk-blue,
with stuff moving in the near still whiteness
going grey behind the blue bands

no pink or rose—that is all below
in black widow concentration
as cave cul-de-sacs still discharge gas
—is the devil such a discharge?
mephitic Mephistopheles?

Astonishing blend of stellar azure and underworld ochre,
congealed brown rash, bruise-violet brown mud,
the scimitar-weave of an allness, bugs and moles on
the möbius-strip of generational push,

deathrow in seedrow,
        Hades as a *colobus satanas*
peering through the stork-hived foliage,

Hades wearing the *colobus* as Hecate wears my mother
rouged and afloat in a bed littered with
the garbage of the hunching, cat-eyed night

The fragile electricity mammality bears
peaks and subsides, finding correspondence in
chestnut leaf towers bushy in the sprinkly atmosphere

Ruins swarm with the veil of romantic poignancy,
they charm us when each burst of grass
            from crumbling walls
should terrify our intentionality

Is imagination not the para(dice)chute,
our bodies the undertow underlings?

I am trying to stay with the geo-hadic lore I can imagine. Motorcycles sew themselves, mortgaged hornets, into the blackness. Birdsong—then, second gear. Another one-eye on the horizontal bone of its cougar-shaft. Under Les Eyzies, my Indianapolis at five years old, our new and only home, a single lot woods next door. My pokings and peeings at the green black funnel stirring under ants. The fresh meat depth of freshly-dug basements. Climbing twenty feet to sway into a range of further green. 1940s northern Indianapolis, Presbyterian yet shaggy. Mystery of mourning doves: invisible neighbors. Rabbit death circulated in the grass; at five, the killer collie was as imposing as a bison. Fecund dark, wildly blank. Adams and Eves flitting the candle-hypnotic pane. Can I come to terms with never waking? And not as if I continue sleeping, but as if all this never was. Massive intricate thingness, the porous absence in this hotel room. Rock shelter room, room whose wall sheltered a man my age 30,000 years ago. Noble entity of absence in which I currently live, a little current, with wandering foetal gaze, inside the hypothetical eternity I will never enter or ever leave

Nothing greater than for a man to give
a daddy longlegs tickle to a receptive source,
to wander weightless over
his beloved's neck and shoulders

Pure loss pours through. I'm home.

[Hotel Cro-Magnon,
June 3, 1987]

A PHOSPHENE GAUNTLET

Phosphenes are geometrical percepts
occurring within the eye,   "closed-eye vision,"
induced by knuckle pressure on closed eyelids,
larvae   uncials,   grading into each
swarming thrones   rose windows   breaking
    sun   a drilled-out black wreath
auraed by a rubblework of light...

I believe Cro-Magnon practiced closed-eye vision
or saw phosphenes, without knuckle pressure,
while confronting cave walls, lamp flicker urging out
amorphisms suggested by cracks   contours
a rich nigredo of dots   zigzags   spirals
intersected by anatomical noticings
    curve rumps   vulva zags   dot volleys–
the animal re-drawn and quartered in phosphene collision,
remembered sightings had to run
        a phosphene gauntlet

          fingered
wall grooves that thudded
back into the gouger
sensations of fingered wounds,
a morpho-sparking channel:
    memory through phosphene to wall
    wall through phosphene to memory,
        fire drill of a finger
rock mind
                    hottest tinder–
inner ignition   initial mind
phosphene and memory
        emery–

LE COMBEL

"the hollow"
                    intestinal
prolongation of Pech-Merle

A 3-foot stalagmitic, cupule-pitted, much polished
   prong
scored my mind with intimations of the Muse

How far back? There is no first
—an African pythoness is feeding a snake
up her vagina, shrieking a gloss of its moves
—a Cro-Magnon is swinging up, and over,
easing this horn in,
does she feel its cold   hiss through her
   "All is transfer!"
Does this pike fill her with premonitions of the Hydra-
   headed tools we all turned out to be?

In the first chamber:
17 red ochre disks and a red lioness
whose body, in death rictus,
arches across the bodies of 3 horses
(who do not appear to be involved,
were they painted earlier? Later?)
The lioness's head is stuffed up into
   the stalactitic bubblework

Below her raised muzzle are slops of red.
For a belly, she has 4 red disks.
Her body attenuates, tiny hind legs nearly horizontal,
as if she's being sucked into...

The painting has a waver to it, as if under water

Network of animal drift electrified by animal spasm

Three more ensembles of red disks,
as if in spagyric relation to
vaginal fissures in the rock:
the first: a large triangle of 36 disks,
the second: like 21 bees, they swarm the alcove,
the third: 18 in phallic loop,
                                        5 more
        curling into 5 more curling out,
        (as in van Gogh's "Starry Night")
They still revolve! Fresh strawberry red,
moist to the eye and tongue

Like Vallejo they possess their coherence

They are prayer-accurate to a kinetic life

Do these disks proclaim that an abyss has been crossed?

That unlike us the other side is gender occult?

That unlike our flesh,
this wall—as we hold our fingers to it—
can sustain our marks
and send them back into our bodies,
vibrations of the end beginning anew in us?

"As they mature, the erythrocytes [red blood cells] lose their nuclei, become disk-shaped, and begin to produce hemoglobin"

Might these disks be a kind of proprioceptive alchemy,
a joining of body to cosmos?

The finite reddening into the infinite?

Surely they have a rapport with animal blood as it glistens and dries to earthworm color, dries to juiceless matter, and surely to menstrual blood–

In the Polish film, *Mother Johanna of the Angels,* it is surely a Paleolithic gesture when the Mother Superior dashes her hand up her white robes, then whirls to the stone nunnery wall, drawing her bloodied fingers down the wall before the alarmed exorcist's face

O mole of me that wants to eat night,
fanged voracity to sink into the outside and hold!

        I lurched into the bunker-like
second chamber backwards headfirst–

A wreath of breast-like stalactites dabbed black.
The Black Goddess? The "breasts" seem part of a tree,
"heavy apple tree foaming with human fruit"
the vertically-split "trunk"   a vulvic fold–
I'm facing the black pods which contain the mead
    we poets hail!

        A rhinogazelgazeliongazelle
caterpillaring,   telescoping out and out

Disks sounding being in bounded space,
binding abyss leaping   to the brain's synaptic gongs

In the neuron orgy
    in cranial dark,
to know thyself is to give a self to no.

BRECCIA CRÈCHE

In this dream, the wraith
raised her lower body, I entered
the cavity of an eviscerated chicken
flooded with bubbling cream and broken teeth,
to awake in Combarelles by Claude Archambeau
pointing out vulva after vulva into which
leaning, headless women disappeared

When a cave makes itself available
as Combarelles did in 1901,
the underworld stands aghast
as life here and now invades

For 95 years
Combarelles has been in psycho-physical subtraction.
Our body warmth produces condensation on its walls
trapping the carbonic gas from our breathing
producing a powdery white precipitate of calcite deposits,
the "white sickness" that nearly destroyed Lascaux

So life projects death into still living images
incised in stone, enlightened stone,
our breccia crèche,
shiftings of the creator infants our fingers
once were

Combarelles is a dream and
a rigid, broken, snake interior
in which I wander,
the mortal nouriture

We men, who bring so little into the world
beyond an orgasmic bumper

to absorb the reassembling of our selves
now in the burn along any edge
touched by our tool-embedded hands.

INDETERMINATE, OPEN

[Parietal human figurations
of the Combarelles cave]

A dorsocaudad line
   hovering
a ventral line

engraved on the tunnel ceiling by someone lying down

Incipient
heaven
   and
earth

•

The human is indeterminate, initially unclosed

•

Thighed female torso
   tangent to
an equine cervicodorsal line

the hybrid contingency

•

Of the elephant hide wall
a particled non-head with triangular eye
supported by a palm and arm wisp of riverine divergences

An immense, flattened breast   floats below,
sunfish through limestone shallows

•

Planted in lifting female buttocks germinating lines,
bearers of thrust,
an erection

•

What is a nodule? Can be a nipple
from which two lines widen
cutting through clay into the limestone,
as if by X-ray,
the vaginal canal is deeper

•

Without eyes
whose nose
only the "carriage of the head"
makes human

•

Mask eyehole observing the back of someone's head
or is that a spider abdomen?
The face side reveals a bald, deer-muzzled geezer

•

A horse's rear leg outlines a woman's upper body,
her torso and head enphallused inside the leg,
her bump eyes staring blindly up

•

Engraved in horse withers,
cambered, breast-angled, seated, graceful

•

On the periphery between nature and human nature,
between unconsciousness and consciousness,
increscent self

•

Upon the altar edge of a huge,
scratched, open vulva
superimposed on a horse's side,
a dorsocaudad female outline places her
why

•

Bending forward, a belly-sagging, bag-headed man,
ithyphallic, gesturing Up Yours—
using his rump for a back line
a one-legged armless half-head turns toward us
as if he is

•

Bag-headed may be giving the finger to
a lumpish dinosaur ghost
shitting as it prepares to mount
a thatch of hindquarters

•

In a horse's belly
a hairy prognath holds out and looks into
the mirror suggested by the jawbone

•

On the fulcrum of a vertical thigh
the dorsoventrocaudad bundle

•

Head and neck wisps of a phantom foetus
up to its sole eye in horizons

•

A huddle of horned vulvas

•

Like sled dogs bounding in slow motion,
animal-snouted archai on the leash of
in the harness of
alchemical mush, moving along Combarelles' Inner Gallery
as if in snowy dust

•

A human erection ascending
as if in circular revolution with
a saiga head descending

As if the 20th century were embedded in that hub

•

Four hybrid judges.
The simian remains moved.
The others—bear-nosed, duck-billed—
bend forward through schist to not
acquit us

•

Armored death's-head with vulvar jaw flaps,
necked,
goateed,
with escutcheon nosepiece,
one eye a pebble,
the other an overturned vulva,
mouthless and
crossed out

[for Monique and Claude
Archambeau]

CLUTCHES

At Skhul, a man died clutching the mandible of a wild boar

At Qafzeh, a child died clutching a deer antler

At Dolni Věstonice, a woman died clutching an Arctic fox

In Paris, César Vallejo said he would die "outside the clock,
clutching a solitary shoe."

In Ivry-sur-Seine, Antonin Artaud died seated at the foot
of his bed, clutching his shoe

In North Hollywood, Lee Hickman died, Charles Macaulay
told me, clutching an issue of *Sulfur*.

DE KOONING'S *EXCAVATION* (I)

To be in the stroke
to be a "slipping glimpser"
to slip the stroke while glimpsing paralysis
            in its metaphorics,
      the cobblestones over tectiforms
   Huitzilopochtli under Dagwood smears

Excavation of where cartoons are parked

Fire spitting between the body parts

Improvisation: oldest habitation

Annunciation at the corner of Carmine Street
the painter looks into the hole:
      there is a way to foal
in dismemberment,   to raft the member-
                  flung wreckage

   Tectiform   Tectiform   roof or sail or
vertical forearm. Add another arm. Wrestling
self is martial meditation–
   no way to begin again? Consider Gauguin:
Europe diseased, Naturalism kaput, trees turned blue,
lizards braided Tahitian Eve. Gauguin exposed
an eco-ethno morass that still shudders.
      His work proclaims:
the goal of vision is a recasting of Genesis–
     end at the beginning

A broken totem descends through *Excavation*:
at top cènter, a bird beak dings (à la Rube Goldberg)
   the roof of a tectiform

whose base is caught like a cocktail tray by
uprushing waiter's splayed fingers and thumb
        —whose cuff bursts into flame!
End of waiter. My eyes continue down, through flexing
diamonds   a pair of braed tits   to a broad tectiform,
    center bottom. This totem midden says:

In the flukes of excavation there is form

The subconscious is coherent

—these lipstick jabs   cleavers   jaw-interlocked
comic heads are a puzzle solved before our eyes

Barely recognizable jigsawed voids become yellow
    semen linoleum
discharging former barely-recognizables

Midden flattened into a painting
"gumspots ... bits of refuse" forced into "bums who lie
    poisoned in vast delivery portals"—
de Kooning's insect-filled night mind pressed
    between two glass plates

Larvatory of lares and lemurs

Gorgon carotid dousing Pegasus

Conundrum of the abstract, more concrete than the real

It invites us to set the primal scene on fire.

DE KOONING'S *EXCAVATION* (II)

Tectiformic anchor sunk in airless kinetic duress.
hexagonal leakage.grainy yolk-and-semen soot-sprinkled
wrench heads clamped on angular holes."ding-busted commotion"
Andy Gump's missing jaw.birdbeak-seized red bolt.zooming
origami bird a pointy-snouted fox inserted in its breast.
interlock and hollow.a deck of shards.firescarred matchsticks
thatched with rats.mayhem jigsawed.vagina dentataed thatches
hatching cats or bats or spats.a candle weeping tent-like
piper pied beauty off the edge.formic cores dunked in deathless
tinny dress.fleshagonal breakage.yoked tan seamen seek red-
headed wench.Cinderella decked by aardvarks.Ed and Esther
trapped by Feds."Vot Der God-Gast—? I t'ought ve vas safe!"
Katzenjammers and Captain in yin/yang scufflespank.hungover
ardor wretching lead.inner rock and wallow.fanged firemouthed
heads.Andy Gump's hissing maw.dill-flecked suet calving melons.
anchor crash on yellowed ivories.Monk-splintered chord.sound
snatched and bricked.haywire hay.a wirey polyscore.ah!uro-
boric exploitation!marigold skullracks shaking with jukebox
glee.Rilke's voracious rusty nail just dying for our soles.
spattered bumblebees recombined with egg white eye whites.
Rorschach of a charred Alley Oop.Andy Gump's hidden sin.
flaming tack sticking through a tit.malarial rage.flagellated
spores.sporozoites locked in cog.anal sprocket halo.disposals
on amphetamine.the plumbing iridescent with Gump's syphilitic
chin. amber hyenasnails basking in rancid deer.a petrified
guffaw. sliding lids of eyes.Wimpy Sea Hag Jiggs and Maggie
chockablock in Adam's pooped Huitzilopochtlian sneer.

BLOODMARE

[for Eliot Weinberger & his
Karmic Traces]

And where might I find, within or without,
that fount or bloodmare, muttering muzzle or
karmic feedback, called the Muse?
Is she around to poke through
the daily smallness of voice, a way
to know more than we actually know,
to clear the rubble packed between a two-chambered
consciousness, so that
the corrosive sublimate,
the phrenia fermenting within phrases,
compost that connect us
directly with our dying, erupts?
At once whirlpool and campanile,
her articulation is inflected by what it quakes.
The poet's inner lining is more than a seasoning.
Whatever passes through me is of my passing
be it radio static or Spicer's martian antennae.
Am I running interference for her
or is she running interference for me?
Xipe Toltec is
the captive's skin,
the priest in a "golden cape" and
the captor in union with the god.
Is my cry a former life
cut off before fulfillment
now trying to sing?
As a ghost in Zeami
crosses the Noh bridge between two worlds,
is one of my former lives
seeking to reverse its fate by realizing
its experience here?

What has been driving me for 40 years?
Night after night I come to what can only be called
the trench I moisten with my own blood,
yet as a sacrifice
it is a keyboard repetition of too many words
for too few goals. The haunting:
that I am ruled by my own missing story
—and do I lay that too on the Muse?

Redbud pods in breeze
reposition a million times an hour.
Something in my brain is raving over being
unable to articulate each shift,
is in short-circuit with the shifting,
is letting something else through the outage,
a kind of splicing, a graft on
the friction, sparking something gnarly
not mine. An earlier version of myself?
The child who did not know mother will die,
is he still here, by that backyard fence,
holding onto the pickets for dear life?

What is it that comes through a "missing child's" face?
Often smiling, much younger in the photo
than when disappeared. Something smiles
in the shadowed eyes. I wonder if it is not
a previous life that, unlike us,
knows what happened to this child...

Did I die, as a child, in a former life?
For I was so reluctant to enter this one—
I waited for a decade before they coaxed me forth.
As an infant I was totally adored
as if they were trying to pull me fully out of pre-
natal reluctance.
Can a foetus create a time warp?

Might another foetus enter that warp?
Might—as I hesitated in the womb—
another life have joined itself to mine?
(When I finally consented to try being here,
my father disappeared into a slaughterhouse,
busying himself with animal death.
My mother was less sure,
often staring at me as if any moment I might replace myself
with an only daughter, or just take off
via their awkward intercourse
back into their desire to justify their lives
before God)

Bloodmare,   yes,   archetypal
cougar chewing my balls.
In the middle of a line
I bite into something that could destroy me,
and it is not a former life outside of Indiana.
It is the hours spent here by back-turned inspiration,
outer-turned hours, image-immigrants turned back.
Are not these hours Bloodmare in mourning?

Where is my childhood now?
Are there 60 of me,
one for each year, facing this typing?
Bent over, side by side, hands touching the floor,
they make a kind of tunnel, tiny
and unable to stand at first, until at 18
the height of their archings remains constant.
How I'd like to run the gauntlet of this extended trope,
seeing my own face upside down 61 times—
I would ask each year:
how was it to be 4? 14?

They'll never say, like
the woman in the dunes who murders most

allowing a few to escape
or the man who tumbled into her lair,
hissing "tell all!" in the woman's ear,
my greed to make it all count,
the anti-greed to let the lived-before
    undergo an acid bath.

IMMERSION

Night covered erection
still unavailable upon waking

To not be
announces daybreak by

dying away

"You are incomplete,
therefore we are attaching the Jesus cradle to your back,
the Joseph weight to your chest,
and here is a Mary candle–

since you asked for everything,
we're going to give you everything
–at once"

Still can't crack, to symbolic
satisfaction, the literality
of cultural background.
But does any American sink the Moses basket,
the babe on the Thanksgiving table
the generations lean toward
like grasper reeds?

Obdurate 4705, inedible prey
trussed in a web. In this maze
I seem to be endless space. Looking at ice,
under which eyes of the drowning beg for their baggage,
I seem to be moving in rock

•

Through the scrotal
density of night I tumbled,
dreaming of Australopithean fingers gripping
zero,
of bags,
of that great bag lady,
the Muse
as mother kangaroo,
a halfway womb house between foetal life
and finitude's domain,
writing while not writing,
no longer pulling the spider sutures
brambling into my clause.

NORN OF PLENTY

Reminded that it was Easter,
I saw the mother of Christ weeping below his feet,
but dreamed that night of my own mother
crucified, myself below her feet—
she hung on so long
I thought the diorama would never bend,
I looked up the body
hanging from huge nails, she was hairy
and not hairy, her brown, wrinkled body was in semi-lunge,
as if to drop on me, paralyzed
by the horror that beat Isaac Babel into a faceless pulp—
as I strained toward her sun glassy eyes,
dream volleys sent torture crises like breakers
through her leaning

As if to drop on me
as if to drop *into* me
to weight me, so that
as a double-backed Beast
we might plunge

A voice said: "If you have the right magic
you can wake from this dream with her soul in your arms,
then you will have paid back
your life, at which time
the Abyss will crystalize with mice"

Then I recalled the oak root
which had penetrated Pech-Merle,
followed it down into the Ossuary,
there it hung, dry and wispy now,
still part of the living oak,
perhaps its deepest root, and I thought of Urd,

the eldest Norn, who lived in the cave
under the roots of Yggdrasil,
said to have drawn strength from Urdabrunnr,
"Urd's stream,"
Urd's menstrual flow?

In this sacred fluid I saw life forms darting,
a puppy, my childhood pet Ginger
who once, while nursing,
looked up at me as just another pup,
was she not my bestial incubus,
my foetal sprite
in fantasy parallel to me
inside my mother?
When I looked into the stream again
I saw a man's face embedded in writhing coal-black pubes,
this "Medusa"
crested like a gorgeous flower in welling blood
now become a moat
bounded by linked gleaming beetles,
all of which were set in a yellow lake
turning auburn, glinting citrus orange—
could I have thrust my hand into it
I might have pulled out the origin of war,
the tiger-headed foetus within man
not yet birthed, a tiger slug
folding in upon itself
a knotted labyrinth,
a compressed Abyss?

The root was in the cave
as I was in my dream,
O fontal Abyss,
non out of which the non-non wavers!
Did the cave "suckle" the World Tree?
Is this Tree, with its Qabalistic zones and paths,

a Yantra of the cave?
The eldest Norn's
stringy dug dangled inches above my open mouth—
what did I take into myself
when I closed about this Malkuth root?
Dust splintered through my throat,
I coiled through myself into the out-stretched
being of Urd,
I was climbing through my mother as she arched
away from that hideous cross,
I was groping about in the richest blackness ever,
these stalagmites, they are her bones,
this tactile dark, her spectral blood

Before me there was a wreath of sparking ochre coals
whose weightless obsidian center
exerted an awful suck—
suddenly the double female fused
and I heard the sound of their fusion as MURDER!
Urd in Mother,
it was the terrific suction of that center,
it was the fallen Norn in rictus to my crawl,
it was my male dread of being sucked
inside an octopodal star

"Angel tripe!"—that voice again—
"Your work is to bring up angel tripe"

And there was Catherine Blake,
in common, dirty dress, sitting in the Blakes'
small room off Oxford Street
bolt upright by her husband's desk.
Her eyes, lowered, fixed on a blank sheet,
her eyes were fiery lasers.
I saw William, off these glowing beams, plucking baby mice.

MATRIX, BLOWER

I was going many ways at once
and did not know the word that was spreading,
a drop of psyche had separated into streams,
each with a febrile image purpose,
ravenous image snakes all heading out hungry for extension,
must one choose
which snake—or might one choose their knotted source?

One says: dream is a stable place to flail,
to swingle bast from circumstance,
and this is almost true

One says: dream wisps are image
produce the poet must pestle
or tie, like a bunch of mistletoe,
dead giveaways, and this too is almost true

This repeated dream: I am crawling a black alley
past sights I cannot bear, alley
intestines, the monster composed of daily news

Last night a nipple was offered—
instead of sucking in the squalor discharge
I wrenched up, banging against a ceiling roar of celebration

I looked back, the alley
now spiraling down to a vanishing

I was inside the horn of plenty
with worm nests for the poor.
Where the fruits of the earth were said to spill,
a slab for the rich
barricaded the cornucopian flow,

the blood issuing from the head of Achelous,
his horn ripped off by Heracles.
It is said that from the blood of this rupture
the Sirens were born–

ragged round pit of the tear,
does it mask the Muse's bloody mouth?

It is also said that Sirens were in the meadow with Kore,
bird-footed bearded girls
watching Kore pluck a psilocybin out of a cow-pie
and bite into its head

–I turned on the sink disposal and heard all forms
roar down,   Kore's screams.
Hadic eruption must have come after
a horn turned Siren

I think poetry exploded from a midden,
overheated garbage, combustion of
all suddenly adding up

Binder Siren and throttler Sphinx
cornucopia down into Muse eggs where inspiration
(the inflation) and fate (the constriction)
separate and combine—

I keep having this fuzzy vision of the psychic head,
of a brain termite queen pumping out image tendrils,
a vision of source hovering as this soft stuff in the skull
and then a creature blowing into it
(Sirens, the nightside or ancient form of the Muse,
are said to suck the breath of the sick
and are associated with siesta-nightmares),
"muse" akin to *musus*, "animal muzzle,"
a Muse-muzzled succubus crawling across the dreamer

or up through the dreaming,
blowing the dreamer's mind,
mind ejaculating into Muse muzzle,
"psyche" akin to "psychein" = to blow

Say Laussel ripped off the bull's horn
and experienced inner tearing
as if something began to bleed within,
what is this thing that was felt?
A killed-out image?
The sensation of a plunging rise,
a fall so total it swerved into ascent?

This bleeding, this fount—
Aztecs saw snakes coiling out a decapitated's neck
not as a fantasy of wriggling veins
but as the body's serpent power
released in the instant of decapitation

To have severed a head
to gaze at life's black, U-shaped power
out of which image larvae began to seethe,
as if in doubling-back depth
there is a fructifying compost equal to
the weight of the loaded horn
which this faceless woman of the nightmare
could barely raise,
feeble left hand resting on her swollen belly,
she now possesses what impregnates her,
she's parthenogenetically cocked

Out of a curdling implosion,
out of a caldron of generational fat,
the Venus of Lespugue rises
and is caught at the waist by
—is it mother flesh

she is ascending through?
As if she would completely pop out, a maiden.
Then I look again: she is docile,
her bowed head dove-like
over a bulbous
double stomach, forearms flaccid.
Buffie Johnson noticed the arms were wing-like,
that Lespugue has tail feathers.
One senses that Lespugue is a frozen instant
where woman breaking into bird
breaking into woman were seized and held,
the pupa of each.
The daughter rises out of the mother core,
bird-shaman invested.
Footless Lespugue—
held upside down, from the back
her pressed-leg-stumps become a head,
buttocks   enormous breasts

    She floats,   Cro-Magnon mind,
frog brain shaped

Like the Venus of Milo, her lackings
project us into her...   chips off the old vulva

Nor is Jeffrey Dahmer
utterly beside the point:
to not want to be left by anyone we touch
    is amniotic—
                        in imagination
we seek to keep our freezer full of heads,
we bow to heads taken before we existed

If nothing is absolutely dead
then all—and nothing—has the power to rise,
like smoke, to permeate me

with its insurrectional deadness

At Abri Cellier: the neck and head of a blowing horse
crudely engraved in a stone block.
Across the neck, a vulva a bit bigger than the horse head
has been gouged.
"The original sentence, the original metaphor: *Tat Tvam Asi,*
Thou art that"
Blowing horse head = vulva,
thus: a blowing horse head vulva,
"Beauty will be erotic-veiled, exploding-fixed, magic-
circumstantial or it will not be"
The *exploding* and the *fixed* at 30,000 BP,
the Aurignacian "hydrogen jukebox."
The vulva is in the head blowing
"to blow" akin to *blowan,* "to blossom,"
to move with force [said of the wind],
to send forth air [as of the mouth],
to be carried by the wind,
to pant, be breathless,
to sound by blowing, to spout water and air,
to force air from a bellows,
to melt [said of a fuse],
to burst [as a tire],
to deposit eggs [said of flies],
to spend money freely,
to forget one's lines,
to enlarge a photograph,
to brag,
to inhale cocaine.
to vomit,
to bungle,
to crack under pressure,
to squander,
to storm,
to play jazz,

to blow a gasket,
to blow blood,
to blow Z's
"I've got to get a blow from this endless surgery"
"My body and my blow get along fine"
"He keeps a blowze and beats his spouse"
"She blew the stoplight at Alessandro"
"A breakfast of blow-out patches, steak, and coffee"
"Her old man was blowin' chow in every direction"
"Two of the mounted force were engaged in the arduous task
  of blowing a cloud"
"I'm going to do the sucker act and blow myself"

Mountains   mammoths   mamountains

Dorsal lines in active penetration of
what I can see through, what I see through with

What I pass is passing through me, the backs
passing through me are passing me back

Rifted tufts of wild cherry, juniper, birch

Clouds heavy with animal membrane,
mortiflies breaking out of seed league,
clouds heavy with marl, with caul, o
the foreloom,   glacier

is inadequate,   reality

is inadequate,   we

are attack admissible, mudderscruf!

The vaginascope is inadequate!

The foetalope, broken!

Tonight I have placed
my mama moth bones in anatomical position,
I have explored the marrow circuit of my credo:
        fetus–
        femur–
        fecundus–
        femina

and I have eaten the guardian spider who,
in carbon mask,
offered herself to me once the bones were assembled

Chords of babycry–there, out there, of wind,
of mooralie

My aim my urn my prattlescream

Once my mother turned herself into a bee with compound eyes
big as plates

Light up the crotch of a scallion

No night was darker with adder inner lushroom

I was 18 months old. I saw my mother give my father a hand job, and said: I can do better than that! So I gave him a blow job. It is hard the first time you get caught. You just agree with Antlered-owl, and say: yes I'm eating my father! He likes it! It is a good thing to do

At what stage are we in our multiphasic Expulsion?

I know the furlough Neandertal extinction has granted

I know reindeer is a plate on which I serve bison

I know I am a plate on which bear serves salmon

That salmon also serves bear
That I also serve hyena

O the chunks of eeling, the hamstrung
natal-ringing
thuds, the icerian
isolation

Divine peak
                    its snow our rivulet
To drink in my buried-alive daughter:
highest altar

"After the first death, there is no other"

Before the first death, was all other?

Can I grasp the news of this newness?

I have eaten my prow,
cradles have sprouted in my nightcoat
—or are they cromlechs?
or birth cones?
or starry sarx?

Passionate Eros suffuses mind in layers of storm mergers

This excites the bears in the void
turning the honey into ransacked hives

Poetry
                "sunyata ryori"
            Emptiness cuisine

It is mind from scratch that leads.

BLUES FOR BYZANTIUM

Clangs of Yeats like blues

Byzantium a stretch-limo
surrounded by
Liberian juju bands of roving infected studs

"dome" a research lab on the Ross Ice Shelf

"starlit" and "moonlit" work for a cruise line

The night-walkers have no song—
they're banged, a mockery of gong

The other night Shade appeared on Jay Leno

"Flames No Faggot Feeds" just cut their first CD

"image" is anything you want it to be

All that cock is   a Hadic bobbin' bough
    crow moisture   mummy seas
the Muse as changeless metal

"scorn[ed]" "common bird and petal"
complexed in midden atmosphere

"dolphins' mire and blood"
    Japanese tuna seines

Green dolphin morgue with chordal seams

        As if Yeats might now hear
        Bud Powell's "Blues for Bouffémont,"

a sanatorium outside Paris, 1963,
a Byzantium abstract

percolating through the changes,
sound-rhymes like winding,
mobile windows, gong and marble,
word-windows facing

walls, images that yet
images beget, scorned, embittered,
Powell in agony of trance, shade more
than man, drunken, abed,

a shape connected to wires,
by electro-shock set in motion,
Calder mobile more than shade,
rototilling while reaping, doors

yielding doors, in the yielding
a window intercedes, revolving,
throwing off arousals
compounded of sacrifice and ooze—

Over a sunken Golgonooza,
an eight-winged hermaphroditic cherub,
Blake hovering—

I lit my palm with Lascaux,
saw Caryl drift across
what had become impossible to see:
origin, love, and contemporary fire in any
  sense of harmony

I lit my palm, by Lascaux's
bird-headed man, saw the image recede
through Egypt's human-headed bird to

Yeats' "golden handiwork"

—the killed-out image hovering,
archangelic toy in late air.

NOTES

Hans Peter Duerr's *Dreamtime,* with its brisk, packed 132 page text, and 237 pages of notes, is a challenging model for the presentation of poetry that is researched and scholarly as well as personal and inspired. Had Charles Olson, say, made use of such a model for *The Maximus Poems,* not only would a "reader's guide" become questionable, but a whole new text might have resulted, a kind of 1,000 page cocoon enveloping the 635 page text. In *Under World Arrest* and *From Scratch,* I have started to investigate such an elaboration, including commentary and information along with the traditional citations. For a 20th century poet, of course, the source of this kind of annotation is T. S. Eliot's Notes to *The Waste Land.* The notion that such annotation is simply bookish or demeaning to the poems themselves perhaps arises from a purist vision of the poem as a kind of mystical flower without a stem, rootwork, or dirt.

Prolegomena: Quotations are from Chapter 1 of Blake's *Jerusalem.* There is a fascinating discussion of the uroboros in Erich Neumann's *The Origins and History of Consciousness.* A differing interpretation of the uroboros is provided by Wolfgang Giegerich's "Okeanos and the Circulation of the Blood," in *Sulfur* #21. Detailed information on Denis Peyrony's excavation of La Ferrassie (a rock shelter in the Dordogne, whose engraved blocks are now in the Les Eyzies Regional Prehistory Museum) can be found in S. Giedion's *The Eternal Present: The Beginnings of Art.*

Reverberations: Phrases from Emily Dickinson's #615 occur throughout the first section. In the fourth section, I quote from Muriel Rukeyser's poem "Käthe Kollwitz." Concerning "Rigoberta Menchu–did you lie?": while my question does not reflect directly on Menchu's testimony (in *I, Rigoberta Menchu,* a harrowing autobiography filled with Guatemalan military brutality), it should be mentioned that even though Menchu's personal integrity seems unquestionable, scholars have pointed out a number of inconsistencies in her eyewitness accounts (see Victor Perera's *Unfinished Conquest*).

de Kooning's *Woman I*: The quotations are from Sahagún's *History of the Things of New Spain,* and Patrick Tierney's *The Highest Altar.*

Unleaving: the title, along with the phrase, "wanwood leafmeal," are from Gerard Manley Hopkins' poem, "Spring and Fall."

Nora's Roar: Both Adrienne Rich and Robert Kelly made perceptive comments on the art of Nora Jaffe, who remains virtually unknown in the art world. Since neither of these notes are in print at this time, I offer them as accompanying angels to my requiem for my dear friend. Adrienne Rich's note served as an introduction to four paintings and two drawings by Jaffe in *Caterpillar* #2:

> *A Note on Nora Jaffe*
>
> Nora Jaffe's art illuminates for me the difference between feminine and female. Nietzsche says somewhere that woman's genius for decoration may be a result of her having for centuries been fated to a secondary role. If the feminine in art is taken as the decorative, seductive genius, the female is something else, a form of potency rather than an amenity or an elegance. (I think of Sappho or Louise Labé in poetry, as contrasted to Marianne Moore or Edith Sitwell.)
>
> In many of her works Nora Jaffe alludes freely to the male body, as to a sexual equal. The femaleness of her art is linked to powerful and assured gestures, strokes of ink or paint possessing the energy of the word *require* in Blake's verse:
>
> What is it men in women do require?
> The lineaments of Gratified Desire.
> What is it women do in men require?
> The lineaments of Gratified Desire.
>
> The power of her paintings is most often a power of draughtsmanship rather than color–draughtsmanship and what strikes me as a richly female sense of the fullness and emptiness of spaces–black and white.
>
> Seduction, in these pictures, is hardly the question–they are not seductive as a more decorative, coloristically idealized art might be. They suggest rather that the kingdom of the body, harsh and beautiful, tense and dreamlike, is a ground where two equals might meet, like Sheba and Solomon; two equals who have been moving toward one another, purposefully, imaginatively, for a long, long time.

In April 1978, a Nora Jaffe exhibition, "Drawings & Relief Sculpture," was presented by the Open Studio Gallery at the Arnolfini Arts Center, Rhinebeck, New York. Robert Kelly contributed the following note to the exhibition catalog:

A Note on Nora Jaffe

The furniture of the mind, like every other, gets creaky, faded, falls out of fashion. The Art Nouveau that gasped back to life for a few moments in the late Sixties, epicentered at Sausalito, leaves a generation hungry for those sexy, sinuous, "organic" forms, but one wisely unwilling to pay the price of elvishness and cutesy that the Raspberry Reich of art demands in these glib days of Commodity.

I want here to hail an artist who startles me with a body of work at once abstract and sensuous. It answers the questions that vex me sometimes: where did a feel for *our* forms go, feel for delicate calf muscle or solid trapezius? Is the flesh just a good idea? Sometimes one wakes up hungry for the simple likeness of humans, even as Ezekiel (maybe) in the torment of exile looked up towards the highest reach of his imagination and saw the Likeness of a Human seated on a Throne.

Nora Jaffe's work is haunted by us. We are the ghosts, *nos homines*, who wander through the vast controlled spaces of her paintings and drawings, who come through the walls of her remarkable reliefs. In her work some Genesis goes further: human made in the image of Image, then world made in the image of human. Image, not shape. Jaffe's work is not representational. It shows us nothing. It enacts from the ground we share: the space we are, and by being in it master and obey.

This is the "human universe" that American poetry has cared so fervently about. And here in Jaffe's work, like Olson's, there is no place that is not us. And that perception, if I'm entitled to it, is the only verbal aspect of her work at all—not a "concept" but a steady conceiving of all of *that* as all of *this*. Appropriation: making ours.

Paradoxes abound. When I first saw her work, like any other child of God I saw cocks and their destinies leaping all over the plane. The in and out of intromission, gothic ogival upvaulting erections out of the longmuscled ardor of leggy forms, svelte bellies—how fine that was, a homecoming for the eye. But at the same time, how clearly wrought these images were in (to me) an entirely different tradition, of Gorky's agonic abstraction, in a structural vitality so focused it could annihilate the figure itself in the burst of what it does. These images do.

Then a subtler, rarer still, sort of tension exists in her work. Two words go over and over in my thought when I consider her big drawings, two words not much yoked together: Elegance, and Energy. True elegance is a shiver, pubic hair coiled on an immaculate sink, a finger pointing to a word in a text, a seventeen day old moon erased by cloud.

Why do I feel so patriotic looking at her work? This is my body, my town. Her work dares me to dissever myself from that community. This is too big for you to get out of. You'll really have to think of some way of putting up with the energy of this system. It says.

And I answer: I love the size of this. It is big in a way that ratifies *Scale* as the fifth dimension of the arts, all arts. I feel it's given back to me (restoration, apokatastasis) the size of what it feels like, what it *is*, to stand in a place and do something there, anything, anything I would wholly do. I feel restored to my own terms.

Another way of saying that is, of course, to celebrate anew that wonderful Absence in this century's art: the banished window. These works are no peepholes, no prosceniums. There is nothing outside. There is nowhere else.

In the poem: the quotation in the first section is from Hart Crane's poem, "Praise for an Urn." Besides *Caterpillar* #2, reproductions of Jaffe's art can be found in #13, and on the cover of *Sulfur* #26. There are also ten of her drawings reproduced in the book we did together, *Realignment*.

Nightcrawlers: For Nancy Spero's image of the mutilated Salvadoran woman, see *Sulfur* #14. The Olson quotation is from the poem, "[to get the rituals straight I have." The Gary Snyder quotation is from his essay, "The Porous World." For "our night crawl through Le Tuc d'Audoubert" see my "Notes on a Visit to Le Tuc d'Audoubert."

Shmatte Variations: Michel Nedjar is a doll-maker, painter, and film-maker living in Paris. His work may be found in the major "Outsider Art" collections in European museums. "Beginners in the world..." is from Rilke's essay, "Some Reflections on Dolls." "Of what does the spider dream?" is the title of a Nedjar film. See *Sulfurs* #26 and #27 for Allen S. Weiss's article on and interview with Nedjar. On the cover of *Sulfur* #37, there is a color reproduction of a Nedjar doll. The most complete presentation of Nedjar's art in book form is to be found in *Les ongles en deuil,* a catalog published by Galerie Susanne Zander, Köln, Germany, 1996, with essays by Roger Cardinal, Chantal Thomas, Weiss and myself. The two quotations that end this poem are tinkered-with entries from *The Larousse Encyclopedia of Animal Life.*

Register's Beyond: the painter John Register (1939–1995) is an irreal realist, a master of a genre of architectural still-lifes, in which realism and the fanciful are blurred. I discovered his work in the home of John and Barbara Martin. This poem was initially stimulated by a Register painting hanging in their living room. Barnaby Conrad III's *John Register* is an introduction to Register and his world.

Notes on Exile and Paradise: "Jewel Spears of heaven" comes from John Lash's *Twins and the Double.* "potent with orphanhood" is from poem XXXVI of Vallejo's *Trilce.* For material concerning "crossing the Abyss," see any one of Kenneth Grant's books on Aleister Crowley and occult traditions. The quotation with which the poem ends is from St.-John Perse's book-length poem, *Exiles.*

Less and Less Wholly Absorbed: This piece began as an argument with Olson's "Wholly absorbed / into my own conduits to..."

Oy: In the quotation, Chaim Soutine is speaking to his friend, Emile Szittya, who wrote a monograph on the painter (*Soutine et son temps*). This comment is translated and reprinted in Maurice Tuchman's introduction to the 1968 Los Angeles County Museum of Art's catalog, *Chaim Soutine.*

Soutine's Lapis: The immediate source for this poem is the 1993 Taschen Soutine *catalogue raisonné,* a revelation for Soutine admirers: it reproduced a number of paintings for the first time, and discarded others (for the most part mediocre works) as fakes. The description of Soutine's "butchershop" (as well as the description of Soutine by Maurice Sachs) is from Pierre Courthion's *Peintre du déchirant* (my translation). The David Sylvester quotation is from his essay "The Mysteries of Nature within the Mysteries of Paint" (in *Chaim Soutine,* Arts Council of Great Britain, 1982). I find it fascinating that not only a painter like de Kooning but one like Register responded powerfully to Soutine's art. In the National Gallery of Art catalog, *Willem de Kooning Paintings,* Sylvester reports that when in 1977 de Kooning was requested to identify his key influences, he said: "I think I would choose Soutine ... I've always been crazy about Soutine—all his paintings. Maybe it's the lushness of the paint. He builds up a surface that looks like a material, like a substance. There's a kind of transfiguration, a certain fleshiness, in his work ... I remember when I first saw the Soutines in the Barnes Collection ... the Matisses had a light of their own, but the Soutines had a glow that came from within the paintings—it was another kind of light." When Barnaby Conrad III asked Register who his favorite painters were, Register said: "Completely unrelated to my own work, an artist I greatly admire is Soutine."

El Mozote: I am indebted to Mark Danner's reportage, "The Truth of El Mozote" (*The New Yorker,* December 6, 1993) for much of the information in this poem.

Out to Show Them: The opening quotation is from Kafka's "Reflections on Sin, Hope, Pain, and the True Way" (in Edwin and Willa Muir's translation which differs significantly from others). The quotation near the end of the piece is from Guido Ceronetti's *The Silence of the Body.* Danniel Hamm's words are from Steve Reich's electronic composition, "Come Out," Odyssey Stereo 32 16 0160. In the liner notes, Reich writes: "*Come Out* was composed as part of a benefit, presented at town Hall in April, 1966, for the re-trial of six boys arrested for murder during the Harlem riots of 1964. The voice is that of Danniel Hamm, then nineteen, describing the beating he took in the Harlem 28th precinct. The police were about to take the boys out to be 'cleaned up' and were only taking those that were visibly bleeding. Since Hamm had no actual bleeding, he proceeded to squeeze open a bruise on his leg so that he would be taken to the hospital."

At Xochicalco: Pre-Columbian ruins between Cuernavaca and Taxco in southern Mexico. The site contains one of the finest ancient ball courts in Mexico. "Woman, your body..." is from a Brazilian feminist poster I happened to see in Mexico City. "The line cut by Adam's black..." is from Vladimir Holan's poem, "Death," the entirety of which (in Jarmila and Ian Milner's translation) reads:

> Once again he is going round
> like the sodden air on an incendiarist's skin
> or the whiff of a nearby brewery.
> I seem him clearly through the line
> cut by Adam's black diamond
> in the glass of virginity.

Gretna Green: This is the name of the street on which Nicole Brown Simpson was living when, along with Ron Goldman, she was murdered. I translated Aimé Césaire's prose poem "Lynch 1" during the O. J. Simpson trial, lines of which made their way into early drafts of this poem. I am also indebted to Césaire's poem, "Le coup de couteau du soleil dans le dos des villes surprises" for its apocalyptic presentation of "fabulous" beasts. The vision of the Beast in my poem is taken from H. H. Lovecraft's *The Lurker at the Threshold* (quoted in Kenneth Grant's *The Nightside of Eden*). The "second animal" stanza quotes form Gary Snyder's poem, "White Devils."

I, Friedrich Schröder-Sonnenstern: Virtually unknown outside of "Outsider Art" circles, Schröder-Sonnenstern (1892–1982) was considered by the poet/art critic Edouard Roditi to be the greatest of the Surrealist painters. Schröder-Sonnenstern's grotesquely hilarious and socially-probing paintings seethe with phantasmagoric fantasy. Surely no other painter ever has made as many visual jokes in his work about the human "ass." The most ample published presentation of this painter I know of is the *Schröder-Sonnenstern* Kestner-Gesellschaft Hannover Katalog 4/1973.

My Evening with Artaud & Othlor: After being offered the Théâtre du Vieux-Colombier for the evening of January 13th, 1947, Artaud prepared some two hundred pages of notes and texts for the event (published in 1994 as Volume XXVI of *Antonin Artaud / Oeuvres complètes*). Nine hundred people turned out for what, depending on one's viewpoint, turned out to be a freak show or a terribly moving manifestation. I conceived my own piece while translating, with Bernard Bador, works from Artaud's final period (*Watchfiends & Rack Screams*). At the same time, I also happened to read my mother's sole diary which she had kept throughout 1935, the year of my birth.

Concerning Section VII: Most of the poems in this section are part of the separate and much longer "Juniper Fuse," a 23 year work-in-progress that attempts to imagine the presence of decorated Upper Paleolithic caves in varying 20th century contexts. Much of the material in this work has already been published, dispersed throughout such books as *Hades in Manganese, Fracture, Antiphonal Swing,* and *Under World Arrest.* Like Robert Duncan's sections from "Passages," these poems belong to the compositional fabric of these books; unlike "Passages," these poems—along with some lectures, essays, and prose poems—make up an "anatomy" of their own.

The Atmosphere, Les Eyzies: Les Eyzies, a small village in the French Dordogne, is the epicenter for Upper Paleolithic caves, rock shelters, and sites, in Western Europe.

Abri du Cro-Magnon: The description of the 50 year old man's skull is from Evan Hadingham's *Secrets of the Ice Age.* The comments on our skull's "disharmony" come from John R. Baker's article, "Cro-magnon man, 1868–1968." Jacques Leyssales, co-owner of Hotel Cro-Magnon, told me that the "cro" in "Cro-Magnon" is patois for "trou" (hole).

Neandertal Skull: I refer the reader to Ian Tattersall's *The Last Neanderthal,* not only for its informative text, but for its extraordinary photographs of Neandertal skulls.

Pleroma: *Webster's New International Dictionary* defines "perichoresis" as equivalent to the Christian "circumincession." I have in mind here a meaning close to that of Kenneth Grant's "interpenetration which occurs between phenomena terrestrial and non-terrestrial."

A Phosphene Gauntlet: Some of the thinking in this poem was stimulated by an article on entoptic phenomena in Upper Paleolithic and South African San image-making, "The Signs of All Times," by J. D. Lewis-Williams and T. A. Dowson. To my knowledge, the word "phosphene" first entered poetry in the Italian poet Andrea Zanzotto's collection *Fosfeni* (1983).

Le Combel: Two small chambers and a stretch of red-disk decorated walls make up the section of the large Pech-Merle cave known as Le Combel. John Lash, in *Twins and the Double,* defines "spagyric" as "the clash of whirling vortices that intersect and spill through each other, generating the perpetual tide-change of inner turmoil that occupies the 'inner space' within dense materiality." Jung occasionally uses the word in his writings on psychology and alchemy. Robert Fludd defined alchemy as "the spagyric art." "heavy apple trees..." is quoted from Camille Paglia's *Sexual Personae.*

Breccia Crèche: Combarelles, with over 600 engravings dated between 13,680 and 11,380 B.P., is several km outside of Les Eyzies. Claude and Monique Archambeau, in charge of the cave for many years, are the authors of a short monograph, *Les Combarelles.*

Indeterminate, Open: This series responds to Monique and Claude Archambeau's photographs and very precise drawings of enigmatic and expressive figurations in their essay, "Les figurations humaines pariétales de la grotte des Combarelles" (which recapitulates Monique Archambeau's PhD Thesis) in *Galla Préhistoire,* Tome 33–1991. I follow the order of presentation in the essay, which begins with the first identifiable representation in the cave and ends with several figures near the end of the Inner (and final) Gallery.

de Kooning's *Excavation* I and II: "slipping glimpser" is de Kooning's 1959 self-description (quoted in the previously cited de Kooning catalog). The "gumspots..." and "bums who lie..." are from Edwin Denby's poem, "The Silences at Night"—which has as subtitle "(The design on the sidewalk Bill pointed out)." I assume "Bill" refers to de Kooning.

In the first poem I tried to identify some of the themes, moods and perimeters that this painting evokes; I then decided that this poem was too stable to come to grips with this nightmarish, cartoonic, and veering work. So I had a second go at it.

Bloodmare: "Karmic Traces" by Eliot Weinberger appeared in the May 1995 VVLS. "bloodmare," as my coined word, is a translation of Garcia Lorca's word, "duende" (often anticontextually translated as "imp"). In his essay, "Theory and Function of the Duende," Lorca writes: "Angel and muse come from without; the angel gives radiance and the muse gives precepts... On the other hand, the *duende* has to be aroused in the very cells of the blood... The real struggle is with the *duende.*" As I read him, Lorca is dismissing the superficial evocations of the angel and the muse of the 19th and early 20th century and attempting to retrieve the ancient and fearsome form of the inspirational which attacks from within (see Robert Duncan's discussion of his poem "Up Rising" in his essay "Man's Fulfillment in Order and Strife"). I suspect that angel, muse, bloodmare (along with sirens and sphinxes) are tentacles of a core force that became available to human beings in the Upper Paleolithic. The three poems that follow "Bloodmare" attempt to envision, study, and particularize aspects of this force.

Norn of Plenty: Urd, Verthandi and Skuld are the three Teutonic divine giantesses said to preside over and determine the fates of men and gods. Collectively, they are known as Norns, or Wyrds (linking them to the Weird Sisters in *Macbeth*). There is a detailed diagram of the Qabalistic Tree of Life in Kenneth Grant's *Hecate's Fountain.* New solid datings for some of the art in the Pech Merle cave reveal that it is over 24,000 years old.

Matrix, Blower: This piece began with my notes on a draft of Jed Rasula's essay, "Gendering the Muse" (*Sulfur* #35), in an attempt to trace Classical Muse formations back to the Upper Paleolithic. An early draft of the poem, "The Inaccessible," appeared in *FlashPoint* #1. To my knowledge, Gordon Wasson was the first to conjecture that Hades' eruption into Kore's meadow might represent an entheogenic implosion (see *Persephone's Quest*). Abri Cellier is an Aurignacian rock shelter near Les Eyzies; it has some of the earliest-known engravings (30,000–28,000 B.P.) in the Dordogne region. "The original sentence..." is quoted from N. O. Brown's *Love's Body.* "Beauty will be erotic-veiled..." is from André Breton's *L'Amour fou.* Definitions and quotations concerning the word, "blow," are from *The Random House Historical Dictionary of American Slang,* Vol. I. "I was 18 months old..." is quoted from Susan Baur's *The Dinosaur Man.* "After the first death..." is the concluding line of Dylan Thomas's poem, "A Refusal to Mourn the Death, by Fire, of a Child in London."

From Scratch begins, in "Prolegomena," by backdating Blake's City of Art, Golgonooza, to include what now appears to be a good candidate for some of the initial moves toward image-making: the cupule-pitted tombstone at La Ferrassie. The book ends with some "blues" based on phrase debris from another eternal city of art, Yeats' "Byzantium." In between, a significant number of poems address works of art and/or artists. In composing *From Scratch*, I kept in mind a sense of imagination that I had picked up many years ago from Northrop Frye's *A Study of English Romanticism*: "it is the power both of creation and response to creation, just as reason is equally a power which can construct or follow a rational argument."

Blues for Byzantium: The second stanza makes use of material from a statement by Tad Homer-Dixon quoted by Robert D. Kaplan in his essay, "The Coming Anarchy" (*Atlantic Monthly*, February, 1994): "Think of a stretch limo in the potholed streets of New York City, where homeless beggars live. Inside the limo are the air-conditioned post-industrial regions of North America, Europe, the emerging Pacific Rim, and a few other isolated places, with their trade summitry and computer-information highways. Outside is the rest of mankind going in a completely different direction." Bud Powell's "Blues for Bouffémont" is the title track of a 1964 record, Fontana FLJ 901. Images as winding windows were first elaborated in my poem, "Winding Windows." "The bird-headed man" is probably a shamanistic figure in a painting referred to as "the shaft scene," sixteen feet below the rest of the Lascaux cave. "Egypt's human-headed bird," also known as "The Soul Bird," is from the XVIII Dynasty and often depicted in underworld scenes on coffins (see, for example, Plate 17 in Rundle Clark's *Myth and Symbol in Ancient Egypt*).

POSTENTRY

8:16 A.M. After writing my Notes, I assumed this book was finished. Then I rewrote parts of "Soutine's Lapis," and wondered about everything else. I reread fifty more pages and decided, no, it *is* finished, and went to bed. It then seems that I dreamed for hours, over and over, of being at a large university for a residency that included several poetry readings. Each time I showed up for a reading I would discover that I had no books to read from, or that the books which some kind soul had taken out of the library for me were in foreign languages. At one point someone gave me a copy of *The Gull Wall*; I started to read from it to discover that I was trying to pronounce Hebrew words and that I was in the midst of someone's prayer. A touching, beautiful woman kept turning up in the audiences, I knew her, did not know her, having had some touching adventure with her that turned on poetry, or about it, I had given her some life words which she had written down and was now trying to find. Like me, she was out of words, or without the words she thought she had. Book after book was handed to me, some with my titles in English, but none of them were my books as I believed I had written them and Black Sparrow had published them. The dream was like the branchings of some great, proliferating tree, each branch becoming a me going out into audience-filled skies, or colosseums where I was to be studied then sacrificed, or sacrificed then studied. Each time I'd show up bookless a 1950s college audience would be there, shuffling about, sitting down, getting up, Cokes in hand. After five years, four thousand worksheets, this dream. Then I think of the right to write, of the fact that no one is shooting at me as I sit here, that if every poet who'd ever lived were to assemble in Ypsilanti and dig my situation they would probably conclude I didn't have such a bad deal. So, I'm not in Bolivia or China and I don't, as Carlos Germán Belli used to, have to carry a few books of mine around in a brown paper sack trying to place them in Lima bookstores. But are my books incomprehensible, can no one read them—isn't that one message of the dream? You say that you write for yourself but that you try hard to communicate this self to others. Well, maybe you try too much. Nobody wants all anyone else has. Are alls poisoned, are some so heavy they feel like nothing? Is my all the empty coal bucket Kafka's bucket rider mounts, or in my case, a book, there I am, riding my book about, hovering over a reader's condo, Hello I cry, it's me, Professor E, I've just completed another book! Another book the interior groans, oh god he's written another one. But no! this one is the best I've ever done, this one will light up the distant horizon and demonstrate how you are attached, or belong to that which is under you, this one will point you at the looney tunes under all you think. Indiana to Lascaux, one fast drive, a single smoking road. Well, the interior replies, that is of some interest, but since attention span has now reduced to dime-thin sauce, what are we do to with you? Your all is now pointless; it may not be a waste of our time but since time itself has become waste, or an immense archeological dump, your contribution is no more than another unleaded can. Postanything, that's the key word, you fill in the blank and hitch it to the Post. Meanwhile, we're inside drinking and gambling with Marlon Vendler and Harold Brando, and it's not that our cards are blank, they're packed with jokers, yet no matter what we draw, the same king always reappears when these low rollers lay down their hands. I returned to my dream. To my inability to have the book I thought I had written. Many in the audience had copies of things that looked like mine, a booked audience that shows up as all authors to hand to the bookless speaker volumes that appear to be his but turn out to be their own prayers. I'd call this blizzard weather, or books as flakes, a gyre in flail: who has come to hear who? Should I stand by podium and listen to the three hundred read from books with my covers but books whose pages are more attached to the audience than to me? Plasmic pages, like loose skin pulled forth, a stomach furl gripped, held forth, and read? Why not? *Read the sun,* I once heard, becoming a poet is the process of learning to read into, around, and through, anything. To read the moon is to imagine the moon. To imagine the moon is to speak as moon. To be a mooner! So the audience is exposing varying parts of their flesh which they read hearing me, or hearing my rustling looking for my book. I read, and they hear me as themselves. Shouldn't that be an occasion of great appreciation, even joy? They experience what I read as part of their own flesh? I am the man I suffered I was *theirs*. But it doesn't work this way anymore, does it? Holding forth a leaf of skin they fail to realize that the words are not theirs, these translators, they hear me as themselves and my presence translated into their pulled-forth selves is, upon translation, simultaneously erased. So my words, which they appear to hear, are translated into their own hopes and confusions, and printed out, or so it appears, for what they hold in their hands is a print-out that "once upon a time" was said to be mine—or at least not theirs, a text between, a table between a me and a you that we used to rest our cases on. So I left the auditorium and looked up a publisher ... it would be easy to be clever here and repeat, with neat flourishes, the author dilemma in a time of commodity. Easy to make jokes, for example: I sold my book on the origin of image-making in Upper Paleolithic cave art by explaining how, in the caves, I had not only lost weight but come to terms with repressed childhood abuse, and as I uncovered this abuse, conspiracy theory was at long last clear: the ghost of JFK appeared in a Font-de-Gaume bison and compellingly narrated how while Oswald was the sole assassin, Oswald was not Oswald but a surrogate mother impacted with Cuban cigars, CIA wiring, and the limbo force of Al Capone's vault. Ruby took care of "Oswald" before this doppelgänger could be disassembled. Actually, Ruby was not Ruby either, but a maniacal distant cousin of LBJ named Strom Hoover. In other words, publisher X told me: anything can be anything as long as it sells. Image has gone into apocalypse. Beast and Scarlet Woman are costumes the natives have abandoned, they are props, as fillable by Hiroshima as by ant-eaters from outer space. Your problem, pub X told me, is: you're still voting in a shack on the Isle of the Blessed. Dope you still believes a mullet is a mallet. So there I was, or here I am, in accord with the industry and still holding my heart in my fist like Verlaine, Rimbaud sneered, clutched a fish. Pub X went on: your absurdity is that of an obsolete white guy; if we could can you we could sell you, but as a heart jumping around like a feverish puppy, the die is cast. It does not matter what you say, what matters is your caste. And just because you're the problem doesn't mean you can harvest some negativity by confronting the system that's produced your crop. Kapeech? What you call imaginative courage is decadence on parade. We both believe an image can be anything. Yours are still strung on transpersonal chains manipulated by your missing story. The images we buy are critic-coded, their stories all reflect existing missings, pop-up audience zones or prestige perks.

So I'm like an alchemist, I guess, an antiquated beaker bubbling away in a Swiss hut, right here, glued to NPR, listening to myself, observing my spider, cooking up a storm, waddling off to teach, translating my baby book, an octopodal radio giving off all the right signals, my flack taken care of, a hopeless case, a cause not lost but encased by too much having been found, an August moon strayed into February, Ariadne's tidbit, Ariadne's clew entangled in the Minotaur's teeth, Theseus slumped drunk in a cul-de-sac, a labyrinth in effect, a sun-oiled tunnel when it comes to night.

On Missing Story Hill, the elves were squirreling away amanita for a journey I had just begun. I watched them work, hoarding vision for a literal launch. Indeed, without this unreadable dream how would I have chanced upon these elfin sties swarming with the flatulence of images-to-be? I was suddenly almost grateful for my fix, babbling away here while Oprah interviews the soul's code. But to leave it at that would be to dismiss my audience reading their own seasonal flesh and accept the auditorium bare. Maybe it always is, for all of us, Smokey Stover included. Maybe the most celebrated author, daisy-chained with readers, stares through these uroboric wreathes as if they are smoke rings, into pointless toil. But maybe he does not. Regardless, here I am, watching on the neighbor's sunny garage front a gargoyle bobbing as it devours its perch. Now, wait a moment, the redbud said: don't mistake my foliage for my fate.

Printed July 1998 in Santa Barbara
& Ann Arbor for the Black Sparrow Press by
Mackintosh Typography & Edwards Brothers Inc.
Text set in Goudy Old Style by Words Worth.
Design by Barbara Martin.
This first edition is published in paper wrappers;
there are 200 hardcover trade copies;
100 hardcover copies have been numbered & signed
by the author; & 20 copies lettered A–T are
handbound in boards by Earle Gray each with an
original holograph poem/drawing
by Clayton Eshleman.

PHOTO: Caryl Eshleman

From Scratch is the twelfth collection of poetry by Clayton Eshleman to be published by Black Sparrow Press. Eshleman is also the translator/cotranslator of César Vallejo, Aimé Césaire, Antonin Artaud, Michel Deguy, Vladimir Holan, and Bernard Bador. Between 1967 and 1973, he edited twenty issues of *Caterpillar* magazine; in 1981, he founded *Sulfur* magazine, currently in its 42nd issue, and based at Eastern Michigan University where Eshleman is a professor in the English Department. He is also the recipient of the National Book Award, a Guggenheim Fellowship in Poetry, and several fellowships in poetry and translation from the National Endowment for the Arts and the National Endowment for the Humanities. Paul Christensen's study of Eshleman's poetry, *Minding the Underworld: Clayton Eshleman and Late Postmodernism*, was published by Black Sparrow Press in 1991.